rororo sprachen
Herausgegeben von Ludwig Moos

Idioms, die bildhaften Wendungen der Sprache, sind der Schlüssel zum Verständnis der fremden Mentalität. Ihr sicherer Gebrauch signalisiert Kompetenz und verringert die Distanz. Das hilft auch im Geschäftsalltag, das Klima zu verbessern. Idioms at Work macht in einer Mischung aus Übungsbuch und Nachschlagewerk mit den «figurative expressions» vertraut, die in den wichtigsten geschäftlichen Situationen die Kommunikation beflügeln können.

Dr. René Bosewitz ist Native Speaker und bereitet in einer deutschen Zweigstelle der London Chamber of Commerce Firmenangehörige auf einschlägige sprachliche Prüfungen vor. Er trainiert zudem seit vielen Jahren Manager aus Banken und Industrie in Business English. Bei rororo sprachen hat er *Better Your English* (60802) und *Perfect Your English* (61147), zusammen mit Robert Kleinschroth *Joke Your Way Through English Grammar* (8527) und *Joke by Joke to Conversation* (8795) veröffentlicht.

Robert Kleinschroth unterrichtet Englisch am Gymnasium und an der Universität Heidelberg. Er hat zwanzig Jahre Praxis in der Erwachsenenbildung und leitete fünfzehn Jahre lang die Sprachabteilung eines Großunternehmens. Robert Kleinschroth hat zusammen mit Dieter Maupai *La Conversation en s'amusant* (8873) und *Flüssiges Französisch* (61184) verfasst und außerdem *Sprachen lernen* (9140) geschrieben.

In der Reihe Business English sind von beiden Autoren außerdem erschienen: *Manage in English* (60137), *Better than the Boss* (60138), *How to Phone Effectively* (60139), *Drop Them a Line* (60261, mit Bryan Hemming), *Get Through at Meetings* (60262), *Check Your Language Level* (60268), *Business English from A to Z* (60269, mit Bryan Hemming), *The Way Things Work* (60369), *Small Talk for Big Business* (60439), *Sell like Hell* (60722), *Master Your Business Phrases* (60725), *Get to Grips with Company English* (60845), *Spice up Your Speeches* (60804), *Better Your Business English* (60846), *Making Money on the Web* (60368) und *How to Communicate Effectively* (61146).

ROBERT KLEINSCHROTH / RENÉ BOSEWITZ

IDIOMS AT WORK

BESSERE GESCHÄFTE MIT TREFFENDEM ENGLISCH

Rowohlt Taschenbuch Verlag

Originalausgabe
Veröffentlicht im Rowohlt Taschenbuch Verlag GmbH,
Reinbek bei Hamburg,
Januar 2002
Copyright © 2002 by Rowohlt Taschenbuch Verlag GmbH,
Reinbek bei Hamburg
Umschlaggestaltung Cathrin Günther
(Illustration Cathrin Günther)
Layout Anne Drude
Satz OCRA und Stone, PostScript Linotype Library,
QuarkXPress 4.0
Druck und Bindung Clausen & Bosse, Leck
Printed in Germany
ISBN 3 499 61333 6

TABLE OF CONTENTS

Idiomatische Redewendungen sind mehr als nur das "Sahnehäubchen auf der Konversation". Viele Idioms sind Sprachfallen für Nicht-Muttersprachler und Ursache für Missverständnisse bei Verhandlungen. Sie kennen jedes Wort, dennoch haben Sie nicht richtig verstanden. Was meint Ihr amerikanischer Geschäftspartner mit "*Let's talk turkey*[1]"? Will er mit Ihnen etwa über Truthähne reden? Wenn man mit Angelsachsen spricht, merkt man schnell, wie reich die englische Sprache an idiomatischen Ausdrücken ist. Dieses Buch hilft Ihnen, Missverständnisse zu vermeiden und Ihre Sprachkompetenz zu verbessern. Blättern Sie es kurz an und machen Sie sich anschließend mit seinem Aufbau vertraut.

Gliederung nach Themen

Dieses Buch unterscheidet sich von allen uns bekannten durch Auswahl und Anordnung der Idioms. Wir haben nicht die übliche Einteilung nach dem Alphabet oder nach allgemeinen Kategorien gewählt. Werfen Sie einen Blick auf das Inhaltsverzeichnis. Sie sehen, dass wir die Redewendungen nach Situationen und Themen aus dem Geschäftsalltag zusammengestellt haben.

Aufbau der Module

Mit dem *Bird's eye view* bekommen Sie einen Überblick über die Unterthemen der Module. Außerdem haben wir sie aus didaktischen Gründen in drei Lerneinheiten gegliedert.

A. *A first taste of idioms:* Als Vorspeise oder Aufwärmphase drei bis vier Idioms zu jedem Unterthema mit sofortigem Schnelltest[2].

B. *The main course:* Dies ist die Hauptmahlzeit, das Kernstück eines Moduls. Jeder Liste mit Idioms folgt ein kurzer Dialog aus dem Geschäftsalltag. Idioms, die manche Angelsachsen als Slang verstehen könnten, haben wir mit (sl) gekennzeichnet.

---

1 reden wir Klartext / sprechen wir offen und ehrlich miteinander
2 Sie werden sehen, dass Sie die Schnelltests (Test your memory) auch ohne Schlüssel lösen können.

C. *Idioms at work:* Wir unterscheiden uns von unseren Konkurrenten vor allem durch den umfänglichen und abwechslungsreichen Lern- und Übungsteil. Sie werden mehr als ein Dutzend verschiedener origineller Testvarianten zählen. Die Lösungen finden Sie in den *Keys* im Anhang.

Zur Erholung bekommen Sie immer wieder *time for a smile* mit englischen Witzen zum Thema. Bleibt noch zu erwähnen, dass manche Idioms Ihnen mehrfach begegnen können, denn eine Redewendung lässt sich natürlich nicht nur einer einzigen Situation zuordnen. Nur ein Beispiel: *be on the bench*. Die Bank kann die Reservebank des Fußballers oder den Stuhl des Vorsitzenden Richters bedeuten. Daher muss jede Einteilung nach Themen subjektiv bleiben.

THE COMPANY
DIE FIRMA

Company is a universal word meaning a collective of people who have come together with the aim of making money, privately and for the company, who want to offer services or products and to be a part of the establishment. But it's not all as easy as it sounds. Companies are always tied up in a lot of red tape put there by governments to make everybody's life difficult.

Bird's eye view

1. Founding companies	*Firmen gründen*
2. Ruining a company	*Eine Firma ruinieren*
3. The end of a company	*Das Ende einer Firma*

A true company anecdote

In the early years of the last century a successful Nottingham cigar manufacturer was approached by a competitor with the suggestion that they go into partnership to produce a new product to be called the cigarette. "They'll never catch on[1]," the cigar manufacturer said. So John Player had to go it alone[2].

Business phrases to remember:
1 catch on: become popular or fashionable
2 go it alone: start a difficult project without help from anyone

A   A FIRST TASTE of idioms

1. Founding companies – *Firmen gründen*

set up shop	*ein Geschäft gründen*
be small fry	*kleine Fische sein*
make a go of the company	*die Firma zum Erfolg führen*

Test your memory: Replace the nonsense word *woggle*

1. Their bookshop was just *small woggle* compared to the modern multi-media markets in the street.
2. Tina and her Toni wanted to *set up woggle* as a bookseller in the High Street.
3. Tina has really *made a woggle* of her shop since Toni left.

2. Ruining a company – *Eine Firma ruinieren*

be up the creek (without a paddle)	*aufgeschmissen sein*
be (in) a shambles	*einem Scherbenhaufen gleichen*
be on one's last legs	*auf dem letzten Loch pfeifen*
kill the goose that lays the golden eggs	*das Huhn schlachten, das die goldenen Eier legt*

Test your memory: Letter mix-up

1. The Board's economic strategy is a *smalbesh*.
2. Since the new legislation came in our firm is *on its salt egls*.
3. We're really *up the ereck* without a new innovative product.
4. By selling the patents the Board is killing the *esogo that yals the golden gegs*.

3. The end of a company – *Das Ende einer Firma*

go bust	*Bankrott machen*
shut up shop	*die Firma schließen*
put up the shutters	*den Laden dichtmachen*

Test your memory: Fill the gaps

1. Many firms will have to ____ up ____ due to the bad exchange rate.
2. The order book is empty. It's time to *put* _____ *the* _____.
3. The socialist laws will probably cause us to go _____.

Time for a smile

Two Scots set up a business and at the end of the financial year they tried to balance the books[1], but no matter how many times they went through the accounts and receipts[2] they were constantly £3.50 short[3]. Finally Jock confronted his partner. "Tell me the truth Angus. Have you been keeping a woman?"

TASK 1: Remember our business phrases in the footnotes?

Replace the words in *italics* by a business phrase.

1. He decided to *do it without help from anyone*.
2. I'm afraid your automatic hair brush will never *become popular*.
3. Magazines often publish short extracts from new novels to *make you buy the book*.

Business phrases to remember:
1 balance the books: *die Bilanz ausgleichen*
2 go through the accounts and receipts: *die Konten und Belege durchsehen*
3 be £3.50 short: *£3.50 zu wenig (in der Kasse) haben*

B   The main COURSE

1. Founding companies – *Firmen gründen*

set up in business	*ein Geschäft eröffnen*
get a company onto its feet	*eine Firma auf die Beine stellen*
create a business out of thin air	*eine Firma aus dem Nichts aufbauen*
launch a new company	*eine neue Firma gründen*
build a company on sand	*eine Firma auf Sand bauen*
go it alone	*es im Alleingang tun*
restructure from top to bottom	*völlig umkrempeln; neu organisieren*
put / set one's house in order	*sein Haus in Ordnung bringen*
be tied up in red tape	*in Bürokratie / Papierkrieg ersticken*
go from strength to strength	*immer stärker werden*
give someone a leg up	*jemandem in den Sattel helfen*
keep one's head above water	*sich gerade so über Wasser halten*
touch / hit rock bottom	*den absoluten Tiefpunkt erreichen*
make a U-turn	*eine Kehrtwende machen*
Making a profit is the be-all-and-end-all of a company.	*Gewinne erzielen ist das A und O einer Firma.*

Idioms overheard

The Financial Director (**F**) is talking to the Managing Director (**M**):

M: So I certainly believe we should *set up a subsidiary* in Italy.

F: It depends when. You know we've *touched rock bottom* regarding cash flow.

M: We have to *get the company onto its feet* and I believe that means attacking a new market.

F: I really don't feel it's the right time to invest. And it's Italy. Think of the *red tape*.

2. Ruining a company – *Eine Firma ruinieren*

back the wrong horse	*auf das falsche Pferd setzen*
support a lame duck	*eine ruinierte Firma unterstützen*
miss the boat	*den Anschluss / Zug verpassen*
be in bad shape	*in schlechter Verfassung sein*
get into a rut	*zur Routine werden; in den alten Trott fallen*
run a company down	*eine Firma herunterwirtschaften*
beat someone to the punch	*jemandem kurz vor dem Ziel zuvorkommen*
get into a mess	*in eine schwierige Situation geraten*
get into hot / deep water	*sich in die Tinte setzen*
be in a scrape	*in der Klemme sitzen*
be in a fix / jam	*in der Patsche sitzen*
go downhill	*bergab gehen*
go down the drain	*den Bach runtergehen*
be caught between the devil and the deep blue sea	*in einer Zwickmühle stecken*
see the writing on the wall	*die Zeichen erkennen*
There's the hitch.	*Das ist der Haken.*

Idioms overheard

Tom (T) and Jim (J) in the sales department:

T: I don't know how long I'm going to stay in this firm. It's *going downhill*.

J: What do you mean? Do you want to resign?

T: Well, our new sales director, he's not doing his job properly. Our sales figures are really *in bad shape*. I can see *the writing on the wall*.

J: But you've got to find another job. *There's the hitch.*

3. The end of a company – *Das Ende einer Firma*

be on one's last legs	*in den letzten Zügen liegen; auf dem letzten Loch pfeifen*
go bust / broke	*Pleite gehen, Bankrott machen*
go out of business	*Bankrott gehen*
wait for the white knight	*auf den Retter in der Not warten*
be up for grabs	*zu einem Spottpreis zu haben sein*
fight a losing battle	*auf verlorenem Posten stehen*
bite the dust	*dran glauben müssen; ins Gras beißen*
swallow a rival	*einen Rivalen schlucken*
be squeezed out of business	*den Hahn zugedreht bekommen*
be at the end of one's line / tether	*am Ende sein; nicht mehr weiterwissen*
go up in flames / smoke	*sich in Luft / nichts auflösen*
close up a company	*ein Geschäft (für immer) zumachen*
Our days are numbered.	*Unsere Tage sind gezählt.*
The sands are running out.	*Unsere Tage sind gezählt.*

Idioms overheard

A discussion between a clerk (**C**) and a secretary (**S**):

C: Have you heard? There's a nasty rumour going round that our company is *up for grabs*.

S: Well, the management is *fighting a losing battle*.

C: So we can only pray and hope for a *white knight*.

S: Who would take over a company that is *on its last legs*. Sometime soon the whole show will *go up in flames*.

A misunderstanding

A businesswoman is sitting at a bar. A man approaches her. "Hi, honey," he says. "Want a little company?" – "Why?" asks the woman. "Do you have one to sell?"

C Idioms AT WORK

TASK 2: Odd man out

Which idiom does not belong in the group? Tick it off and translate it.

1. **A.** set up shop
   B. close up shop
   C. shut up shop
   _____

2. **A.** kill two birds with one stone
   B. kill one's cash cow
   C. kill the goose that lays the golden eggs
   _____

3. **A.** be in deep water
   B. get into a rut
   C. get into hot water
   _____

4. **A.** go bust
   B. go broke
   C. go downhill
   _____

TASK 3: Body language

Replace the *woggle* with a *part* or an *activity* of the body.

1. Last year our little grocery was on its last *woggles*.
2. We were fighting a losing battle to keep our *woggles* above water.
3. We tried everything to get the business onto its *woggles* again.
4. However, all of our great ideas to rescue it *woggled* the dust!
5. We were up for grabs and almost *woggled* up by TallWart, a chain of supermarkets.
6. Then the white knight, the software giant SIP, appeared and gave us a *woggle* up in the form of a generous loan.

TASK 4: Tim, the 'Yes-man'

Tim echoes Tom using an idiom that has the same meaning as Tom's words in *italics*.

1

Tom: If we don't apply for funding now, we'll probably *have no chance of getting any.*

Tim: Absolutely! We mustn't _____ the _____.

2

Tom: It was a *mistake to support the Afghanistan project.* We're losing a lot of money.

Tim: You're right. *We're* _____ the wrong _____.

3

Tom: A single mistake, and all our investments in Kabul would be lost forever.

Tim: You're right as always, Tom. All the money would *go* _____ the _____.

4

Tom: *There is not much time left:* we must get our money out of that country by the end of next week.

Tim: Yes, indeed, *the* _____ *are* _____ out.

5

Tom: Of course, this would mean a *complete change in strategy.*

Tim: Yes, *a spectacular* _____ .

6

Tom: By the way, our office building is starting to degenerate. Even the walls are crumbling.

Tom: Yes, everything here *is going* _____ .

7

Tom: And the entire office equipment *breaks down every second day* because we haven't got the money to replace it.

Tim: Yes, it's really depressing. Everything here is *on its* _____ .

8

Tom: If we can't raise a million pounds our *company will go bankrupt.*

Tim: Yes, we'll *go* _____ , if we can't find the money.

9

Tom: Let's be realistic. The Afghanistan connection was an *illusion which has resulted in failure.*

Tim: Yes, let's face it! All our projects have clearly *gone* _____ in
_____ .

10

Tom: I'm afraid of *a hostile takeover.* Anybody could buy us for a song.

Tim: Yes, indeed. Our company might already *be* ____ for _____.

11

Tom: And there's no bank in the world *that would be ready to save us* from this dangerous situation.

Tim: Yes, we're waiting in vain for a _____ _____ to rescue the company.

LERNTIPP : Bite (on) the bullet

First the bad news: Das Englische ist eine Sprache mit vielen Idioms. Wer sie nicht beherrscht, gerät in Gefahr, Situationen misszuverstehen. Vorsicht beim Gebrauch von Idioms. Beherrscht man sie nicht exakt Wort für Wort, wird man als Ausländer belächelt. In den sauren Apfel beißen heißt eben nicht *to bite into the sour apple,* sondern *bite on the bullet* (Patrone).

And now the good news: Viele idiomatische Ausdrucke sind sprachliche Bilder, die sich gut einprägen, wenn man sie in mentale Bilder verwandelt. Zum Beispiel: *bite on the bullet.* Stellen Sie sich vor, wie sie auf (*on*) eine große *bullet* beißen, die sauer schmeckt. Je grotesker Ihr Bild, desto einprägsamer ist es.

THE TOP FLOOR
DIE CHEFETAGE

Companies consist of workers, specialists, managers and bosses. In theory the bosses should manage the employees and give them directions. The boss should also make the strategic decisions which should lead the whole company to success. But he's only human, too. To err is human[1].

Bird's eye view

1. What it means to be the boss	*Was es heißt, Chef zu sein*
2. Working as a boss	*Als Chef arbeiten*
3. Handling subordinates	*Umgang mit Mitarbeitern*
4. Handling bosses	*Umgang mit Chefs*
5. Firing a boss	*Einen Boss feuern*

Time for a smile

"My son Tom is so forgetful," complained the boss to his secretary. "I asked him to get me a packet of cigarettes on his way back from lunch, but I'm not even sure he'll remember to come back himself." A few minutes later Tom dashed into the office, shouting: "Dad! At lunch I met old man Kelly, who hasn't ordered a penny's worth from[2] us in five years and before we parted I'd talked him into a half-a-million-dollar order[3]!"

"What did I tell you?" sighed the boss, "he's forgotten the cigarettes!"

Business phrases to remember:

1 To err is human: *Irren ist menschlich*
2 not to order a penny's worth from someone: *für keinen Pfennig bestellen*
3 talk someone into an order: *jemandem einen Auftrag abschwatzen*

A   A FIRST TASTE of idioms

1. What it means to be the boss – *Was es heißt, Chef zu sein*

be as hard as nails	*knochenhart sein*
sit firmly in the saddle	*fest im Sattel sitzen*
rule the roost	*Herr im Haus sein; das Zepter in der Hand halten*
roll out the red carpet; give someone the red carpet treatment	*den roten Teppich für jemanden ausrollen*

Test your memory: Missing letters

1. When the mayor arrived at our company we gave her the *r_d c_rp_t tr_ _tm_nt.*
2. Mr Moodan is *sitting firmly in the s_ddl_* at Dutch Bank. There's no real competition for him there.
3. To look at our secretary you'd think butter wouldn't melt in her mouth[1], but in fact she's *as _ _ rd as _ai_ _.*
4. His words are law at CBI. He *r_l_s the r_ _ st* with an iron fist.

2. Working as a boss – *Als Chef arbeiten*

hire and fire staff	*Personal heuern und feuern*
make a snap decision	*eine spontane Entscheidung treffen*
pull strings	*die Fäden in der Hand haben*
be left holding the baby	*der Dumme sein; eine Sache am Hals haben*

Test your memory

1. We bought a bad company and in the end we were left _____ the _____.

....

A phrase to remember:
1 butter wouldn't melt in her mouth: *sie kann kein Wässerlein trüben*

2. The Board made a _____ _____ to swallow a small competitor[1]. I hope it was the right one.

3. Our director is always somewhere in the background _____ _____ to support the business.

4. When we think of America, we think of the policy of _____ and _____ staff.

3. Handling subordinates – *Umgang mit Mitarbeitern*

go over someone's head	*über jemandes Kopf hinweg etwas tun*
like it or lump it	*sich etwas wohl oder übel gefallen lassen (müssen)*
put one's foot down	*hart durchgreifen; ein Machtwort sprechen*
bite someone's head off	*jemandem den Kopf abreißen*

Test your memory: Find the mistake

1. I've told you people you simply have to finish this contract in time, *foot it or lump it.*

2. I'm fed up with shabby work. I'll *put my head off* once and for all.

3. I asked our department leader for a day off[2] and *he put my head off.*

4. A clerk in the patent department decided to *go over his boss's foot* to the technical director.

4. Handling bosses – *Umgang mit Chefs*

pay lip service to	*ein Lippenbekenntnis ablegen*
soft-soap someone	*jemandem schmeicheln; Honig um den Bart schmieren*
kick somebody upstairs	*jemanden auf ein Abstellgleis befördern*
put out to pasture / grass	*in den Ruhestand versetzen*

Business phrases to remember:
1 swallow a competitor: *einen Konkurrenten schlucken*
2 ask for a day off: *um einen Tag Urlaub bitten*

Test your memory

1. The employees don't work correctly. They only _____ _____ service to the boss.

2. He's nothing but trouble. That's why the Board _____ him _____.

3. As soon as the technical director reached 58 he was _____ out to _____.

4. She's a slippery character. She believes the only way to success is to _____ - _____ her boss.

Time for a smile

The company has been expanding on the home market, so the boss invited his sales team into his office. "You have done so well that I'm giving you all cheques for $1,500," he said, and on second thoughts[1] he added, "if you keep on working like this, I might even sign them."

A business phrase to remember

1 on second thoughts: *nach reiflicher Überlegung, wenn ich es mir recht überlege*

B — The main COURSE

Roll up your sleeves, and get down to it[1]

1. What it means to be the boss – *Was es heißt, Chef zu sein*

be a big shot / noise	*ein hohes Tier sein*
be a fat cat	*ein Bonze sein*
be top dog	*der Platzhirsch / Stärkste sein*
be a big fish in a small pond	*zu den Honoratioren zählen*
belong to the upper crust	*zu denen da ganz oben gehören*
be in the driver's seat	*die Firma lenken*
take the reigns	*das Steuer in die Hand nehmen*
have the say	*das Sagen haben*
be in the limelight	*im Rampenlicht stehen*
It's all chiefs and not enough Indians.	*Es gibt nur Bosse und keine Arbeiter.*
think one is the cat's whiskers	*sich für was Besonderes halten*
carry weight with the government	*Einfluss auf die Regierung haben*
get away with (blue) murder	*sich jeden Unfug erlauben können*

 Idioms overheard

Two employees in the R & D department, Ted (**T**) and Paul (**P**):

T: Well, I have to say that things have really been looking up[2] since Dr Spiegel took over.

P: I agree. He *sets the tone* and gets things done.

T: Well, somebody certainly has to *be in the driver's seat* and take on the challenge.

P: And personally I think he loves *being in the limelight*.

Business phrases to remember:
1 Roll up one's sleeves, and get down to it: *die Ärmel hochkrempeln und in die Hände spucken*
2 things have been looking up: *die Situation hat sich verbessert*

2. Working as a boss – *Als Chef arbeiten*

have one's finger on the pulse of history	*den Finger am Puls der Zeit haben*
be in the know	*eingeweiht sein; Bescheid wissen*
run the show	*den Laden schmeißen*
call the shots	*lenken; entscheiden, wo's langgeht; das Sagen haben*
pull the strings	*die Fäden in der Hand halten; Beziehungen spielen lassen*
give the nod to	*einer Sache grünes Licht geben; befürworten; etwas abnicken*
call the tune	*den Ton angeben; die erste Geige spielen*
get one's own way	*seinen Willen bekommen; tun können, was man will*
carry the can	*die Verantwortung tragen; den Kopf hinhalten*
face the music	*sich der Verantwortung stellen; die Suppe auslöffeln*
shoulder the blame / burden	*die Schuld auf sich nehmen*
take charge of	*etwas in die Hand nehmen*
cop out	*sich (vor einer Pflicht) drücken*
get back in harness	*die Geschäfte wieder übernehmen; die Zügel wieder in die Hand nehmen*
work around the clock	*rund um die Uhr arbeiten*
burn the midnight oil	*bis spät in die Nacht arbeiten*
drag one's feet	*Verzögerungsstrategie betreiben; sich reichlich Zeit lassen*
act behind the scenes	*hinter den Kulissen agieren*
have one's fingers in many pies	*überall seine Hand im Spiel haben*
take steps	*Schritte unternehmen*
take action	*tätig werden; in Aktion treten*

Idioms overheard

Jean (J) and Liz (L), two secretaries, are talking about their boss:

J: I'm not too happy about the way Tom is managing this office. I think he's *dragging his feet* a bit.

L: Right. You never know what he's doing. He's *got his fingers in a lot of pies* and you always have the feeling he's *acting behind the scenes*.

J: Well, if he *cops out* on his results he'll have to *face the music* and find a new job.

3. Handling subordinates – *Umgang mit Mitarbeitern*

The good boss	*Der gute Chef*
place someone in charge of	*jemandem Verantwortung übertragen*
give someone the green light	*jemandem grünes Licht geben*
give / get the thumbs up	*grünes Licht geben / bekommen*
give a boost to	*jemanden (moralisch) aufmuntern*
grant / do someone a favour	*jemandem einen Gefallen tun*
pull a few strings for someone	*seine Beziehungen für jemanden spielen lassen*
be in someone's good books; be well in with someone	*bei jemandem einen Stein im Brett haben*

The strict boss	*Der strenge Chef*
get someone moving	*jemandem Beine machen*
keep a tight reign on	*am kurzen Zügel führen*
pile work onto somebody	*jemanden mit Arbeit überhäufen*
keep someone on the trot / go	*jemanden in Trab halten*
rush somebody off their feet	*jemanden ständig auf Trab halten*
rule with a rod of iron; rule with an iron fist	*ein strenges Regiment führen; mit eiserner Hand regieren*
pile the pressure on	*jemanden unter Druck setzen*
straighten someone out	*jemandem den Kopf zurechtrücken*
give someone a lecture	*jemandem eine Standpauke halten*
give someone the thumbs down on something	*etwas ablehnen; verwerfen*

call someone on the carpet	*sich jemanden zur Brust nehmen*
call someone to account	*jemanden zur Rechenschaft ziehen*
get the whip hand of someone	*die Oberhand gewinnen über jemanden*
give someone a hard time	*es jemandem schwer machen*

The unpleasant boss — *Der unangenehme Chef*

be in someone's bad books	*bei jemandem schlecht angeschrieben sein*
crack down on someone	*harte Maßnahmen gegen jemanden ergreifen*
boss someone around	*jemanden herumkommandieren*
keep someone in the dark	*jemanden im Dunkeln lassen*
haul someone over the coals	*jemandem aufs Dach steigen*
read someone the riot act	*jemandem die Leviten lesen*
use the carrot and the stick	*mit Zuckerbrot und Peitsche behandeln*
give someone a dressing-down / ticking-off	*jemanden zur Schnecke machen; jemandem eine Standpauke halten*
pass the buck	*jemandem den Schwarzen Peter zuschieben*
bring to heel	*in die Knie zwingen*
give someone the run-around	*jemanden unnötig hin und her schicken*
crack the whip	*die Peitsche schwingen*
tear a strip off someone	*jemanden zusammenstauchen*
give a going-over to someone	*jemanden runterputzen*
put someone through the mangle	*jemanden in die Mangel nehmen*
It's thumbs down to your request!	*Ihre Bitte ist abgelehnt!*
give a licking to	*eine Abreibung verpassen*

Time for a smile

A born executive is someone
whose father owns the company.

Idioms overheard

The personnel director (**P**) in discussion with the head of IT (**I**):

P: So, some of the people in your department are complaining that they *are being rushed off their feet* and that you are *piling work onto* them. They've no chance.

I: They are right. There is a lot of work. And some people are not doing their bit. I had to *tear a strip off* one of them last week.

P: I understand you've got to discipline them. But what about *using the carrot and the stick*? Listen, ...

4. Handling bosses – *Umgang mit Chefs*

be at someone's beck and call	*nach jemandes Pfeife tanzen*
pay lip-service to someone	*jemandem nach dem Mund reden; Lippenbekenntnisse machen*
give a big hand to	*jemandem lebhaften Beifall spenden*
take the bull by the horns	*den Stier bei den Hörnern packen*
eat out of someone's hand	*jemandem aus der Hand fressen*
bow and scrape	*katzbuckeln; Kratzfüße machen*
soft-soap someone	*jemandem Honig um den Bart schmieren*
toady to someone	*vor jemandem kriechen / Rad fahren*
lick someone's boots	*jemandem die Stiefel lecken*
be a creep	*eine Radfahrer sein*
kiss someone's ass (sl)	*jemandem in den Hintern kriechen*
play second fiddle	*die zweite Geige spielen*
blow / let off steam	*Dampf ablassen*
rub elbows / shoulders with someone	*jemandem nahe stehen; auf du und du sein mit jemandem*
know one's place	*wissen, was sich gehört; sich einzuordnen wissen*

5. Firing a boss – *Einen Boss feuern*

kick someone upstairs	*jemanden durch Beförderung kalt-stellen*
give someone the golden handshake	*jemandem das Ausscheiden vergolden*
give someone a dead end job; give someone a no-hope job	*auf ein Abstellgleis fahren / schieben*
ease someone out	*jemanden loswerden*
put out to pasture / grass	*in den Ruhestand versetzen*
kick out a shareholder	*einen Teilhaber ausbooten*

 Idioms overheard

Two clerks, Sue (**S**) and Jane (**J**), are talking about a colleague and their boss:

S: The way Linda *soft-soaps* Mr Bloggs really makes me angry. She has *him eating out of her hand*.

L: I think she's after his job. She's *licking his boots* to *ease him out* later somehow.

S: Well, we'll have to warn him. I wouldn't want Linda as my boss, would you?

Time for a smile

"My son-in-law has joined my clothing business, and yesterday I caught him kissing one of the models."
"Well, so what?"
"You don't understand – I make men's clothes!"

C Idioms AT WORK

TASK 1: Bosses and the kingdom of animals

Replace the *woggle* with a suitable animal word.

1. Dr Block is rich and powerful. He is the fat *woggle* in our business.
2. He knows he is superior to others and he's determined to show that he's still (the) top *woggle* in the company.
3. Dr Block is an important and influential person. In our small village he is a big *woggle*.
4. All in all Dr Block has a high opinion of himself. He thinks he's the *woggle's* whiskers.
5. He rules the *woggle* because he's the dominant person in the firm.
6. Let's see how long he will be able to sit firmly in the *woggle*.

TASK 2: Test your business phrases

Fill in a suitable business idiom.

1. She appears innocent, although she is probably not.
   She looks as if _____ wouldn't _____ in her _____ .
2. Let's get down to work: Let's _____ up our _____ .
3. His boss was on a trip, so Peter had to deal with the police.
   Peter was left _____ the _____ .

TASK 3: Idioms that make a noise

Complete the sentences using words from the table.

play	steam	face	tune
let	music	call	fiddle

1. I have no intention of _____ to the new boss, so I'll resign.
2. He has been caught cheating, now he must _____.
3. The children were out in the playground _____.
4. You're not the man to _____. You are not in a position to control the situation.

TASK 4: Magic squares – Body idioms

Match the phrases (1, 2, 3) with the parts of the body (A, B, C). Put the numbers in the magic squares. Columns and rows will all add up to the same number, **15**.

A. heel	D. leg	G. head
B. foot	E. lip	H. shoulders
C. finger	F. hand	I. thumb

1. The boss had to put his ★ down to stop the waste of money.
2. Thank god the boss is on holiday. I hate being under his ★.
3. If I hadn't given him a ★ up he wouldn't have landed this job.
4. A boss shouldn't go over everybody's ★ and do everything alone.
5. He's a real creep – always paying ★ service to the boss.
6. A good executive has his ★ on the pulse of history.
7. A good secretary has her boss eating out of her ★.
8. The CEO has been trying in vain to bring the strikers to ★.
9. Twice a week our boss has to rub ★ with journalists and politicians.

A =	B =	C =
D =	E =	F =
G =	H =	I =

PERSONNEL MATTERS
PERSONALANGELEGENHEITEN

Well, it's all about the tasks of personnel. And there are a lot! They have to find the right employees, train them so that the company achieves its goals[1], and so that the employee feels that he is important and can get his optimal training. Personnel has to evaluate[2] them, and if necessary, give them their walking papers[3] if it doesn't work out. Once again it's a problem of interpersonal skills. A difficult job!

Bird's eye view

1. Hiring and firing	*Einstellen und Entlassen*
2. Training and learning	*Ausbildung und Lernen*
3. Assessing and criticising	*Beurteilen und Kritisieren*

Ads that went wrong

Wonderful opportunity for young woman to join fishing partners. Must be able to cook, wash. Please send photo of boat.

Man wanted to wash dishes and two waitresses.

Business phrases to remember:
1 achieve goals: *Ziele erreichen*
2 evaluate employees: *Angestellte beurteilen*
3 give a worker his walking papers: *einem Arbeiter seine Papiere geben / ihn entlassen*

A — A FIRST TASTE of idioms

1. Hiring and firing – *Einstellen und Entlassen*

short-list applicants	*Bewerber in die engere Auswahl nehmen*
put someone through his paces	*jemanden auf Herz und Nieren prüfen*
land a plum job	*einen Traumjob ergattern*
give someone the boot (sl)	*jemanden feuern*

Test your memory: x stands for a/e/i/o/u

1. I was *shxrt-lxstxd* for the job but I didn't get it.
2. He didn't get results so he *was gxvxn the bxxt*.
3. She was lucky, she *gxt a plxm jxb* at the BBC.
4. The applicants will be *pxt through thxxr pxcxs* by experienced interviewers.

2. Training and learning – *Ausbildung und Lernen*

learn the ropes	*die Kniffe / Tricks lernen*
get the knack	*den Bogen herauskriegen*
be in the picture	*im Bilde sein*

Test your memory

1. Now that you've explained how it works in the Personnel Department I'm *in the* _____.
2. Making pancakes is easy once you've *got the* _____ of it.
3. She's just joined the department[1] – it'll take her a week or two to *learn the* _____.

Business phrases to remember:
1 join a department: *in eine Abteilung kommen / eintreten*

3. Assessing and criticising – *Beurteilen und Kritisieren*

get one's act together	*sich zusammenreißen*
be head and shoulders above the rest	*den anderen haushoch überlegen sein*
make the best of a bad job	*das Beste aus einer Sache machen*

Test your memory: Two mistakes in each sentence. Correct them!

1. Mr Klein is *had and shoulder* above the rest of the department.
2. I know it's not what you wanted, but you have to *cake the best of a sad job*.
3. If you want to get promotion you'll have to *get one's tact together*.

Time for a smile

Holiday is the spare time you grant[1] your employees to remind them of the fact that the company can survive without them.

---

1 grant someone spare time: *jemandem Freizeit gewähren / frei geben*

B   The main COURSE

1. Hiring and firing – *Einstellen und Entlassen*

count heads / noses	*Köpfe zählen; die Zahl der Mitarbeiter feststellen*
fill a vacancy	*eine freie Stelle / Posten besetzen*
contact a head-hunter	*einen Personalberater für die Suche nach Führungskräften kontaktieren*
be on the short list	*in der engeren Auswahl stehen*
draw up a short list of applicants	*Bewerber in die engere Auswahl nehmen*
offer a steady job	*eine sichere Arbeitsstelle anbieten*
mention the perks	*die Leistungsanreize erwähnen*
That's right up my street.	*Das ist genau das Richtige für mich.*
That's my line of business.	*Das ist ganz mein Fall.*
not be up to the mark for the job	*nicht das Zeug für eine Stelle haben*
give someone a desk job	*jemandem einen Schreibtischjob geben*
separate the sheep from the goats / the wheat from the chaff	*die Spreu vom Weizen trennen*
Heads will roll!	*Da werden Köpfe rollen!*
scrape (the bottom of) the barrel to fill a vacancy	*verzweifelt versuchen, eine Stelle zu besetzen*
If you pay peanuts you get monkeys.	*Qualität hat ihren Preis; von nichts kommt nichts.*
Good workers are far and few between.	*Gute Arbeiter sind spärlich gesät.*
There are plenty other fish in the sea.	*Ich kann an jedem Finger zehn (Bewerber) haben.*
give the push / sack / chop / bounce (sl)	*jemanden feuern*
get the axe / boot (sl)	*gefeuert werden*
sack / fire / axe someone (sl)	*jemanden feuern, rauswerfen*

give someone a leaden hand-shake	*jemanden mit einer mageren Abfindung entlassen*
give an employee his walking cards / papers	*jemandem die Papiere geben / ihn entlassen*
be at a loose end	*beschäftigungslos sein; in der Luft hängen*
be the work horse of the company	*das Arbeitspferd der Firma sein*

Idioms overheard

Two clerks in the sales department of HM Concrete, Manuela (**M**) and George (**G**):

M: I don't think it's very fair what happened to Tom. He was *given his cards* without any notice.

G: Right, but I guess he deserved it. He *wasn't up to the mark.*

M: I know there *are plenty of other fish in the sea.* But nevertheless!

G: Well, a department leader's job is a hard job. It certainly *separates the wheat from the chaff.* But then it's also a well-paid job. That's life!

2. Training and learning – *Ausbildung und Lernen*

show willing	*guten Willen zeigen*
bite the bullet and try one's best	*die Zähne zusammenbeißen und sein Bestes versuchen*
learn one's lesson	*seine Lektion lernen*
show someone the ropes	*jemandem die Regeln / Kniffe zeigen*
learn the hard way	*aus schlechten Erfahrungen lernen*
get one's hand in	*sich eingewöhnen; wieder in Übung kommen*
keep one's hand in	*in Übung bleiben*
get the hang of something	*den richtigen Dreh finden; den Bogen rausbekommen*
turn one's hand to something	*sich einer Sache zuwenden*
put someone in the picture	*jemanden ins Bild setzen*

take something in one's stride	*etwas mit Leichtigkeit schaffen*
make the grade	*es schaffen; das Niveau erreichen*
pass an exam with flying colours	*eine Prüfung mit Glanz und Gloria bestehen*
throw pearls before the swine	*Perlen vor die Säue werfen*
Once bitten twice shy.	*Gebranntes Kind scheut das Feuer.*
You can't make a silk purse out of a sow's ear.	*Aus einem Kieselstein kann man keinen Diamanten schleifen.*
You can lead a horse to water, but you can't make it drink.	*Mit Gewalt lässt sich (bei ihm / ihr) nichts erreichen.*
You can't teach an old dog new tricks.	*Was Hänschen nicht lernt, lernt Hans nimmermehr.*

Food for thought

Most young blokes stop looking for work
the moment they get a job.

❖

"Are you looking for work , young man?"
"No, but I wouldn't mind a job."

Idioms overheard

Personnel manager (**P**) in discussion with department leader (**D**):

P: So, what's your opinion? Can she *learn the ropes* in the business?

D: Well, *she's a greenhorn*, but she's very motivated. And she's obviously *passed her exams with flying colours.*

P: Okay. She *shows willing* so we ought to give her a chance. Now to the question of salary.

3. Assessing and criticising – *Beurteilen und Kritisieren*

(not) judge a book by it's cover	*(nicht) nach dem Schein beurteilen*
raise someone's spirits	*jemanden aufmuntern*
fall behind with one's work	*mit seiner Arbeit in Rückstand geraten*
catch an employee napping	*einen Angestellten bei etwas erwischen / überraschen*
fall down on the job	*nicht die Erwartungen erfüllen*
read someone like a book	*jemanden wie ein offenes Buch lesen*
hold (it) against somebody	*jemandem etwas vorhalten / vorwerfen*
give someone a piece of one's mind	*jemandem gründlich die Meinung sagen*
give someone a rough ride	*jemanden scharf kritisieren*
give someone the third degree	*jemanden in die Mangel nehmen*
His heart is not in his work.	*Er ist mit dem Herzen nicht bei der Sache.*
let something slide	*etwas schleifen lassen*
He's a dead loss.	*Er ist ein totaler Versager.*
be fair to middling	*leidlich; so lala; mittelprächtig sein*
She dots the "i"s and crosses the "t"s.	*Sie erledigt ihre Aufgaben mit peinlicher Genauigkeit.*
(not) be able to hold a candle to somebody	*jemandem (nicht) das Wasser reichen können*
be cut out for something	*für etwas wie geschaffen sein*
be a dab hand at something	*ein goldenes Händchen bei etwas haben; etwas aus dem Effeff können*
praise to the skies	*über den grünen Klee loben*
be head and shoulders above the rest	*den anderen haushoch überlegen sein*

Idioms overheard

Personnel manager (**P**) in discussion with department leader of production (**D**):

P: So, what you're saying is that John Smith has *fallen down on the job*.

D: It's not that, but *his heart's not in the work*. He's got personal problems.

P: Well, we all have personal problems. But if *someone's not cut out for the work* he shouldn't take on a job like that.

D: Oh, sometimes it's not that easy.

Time for a smile

"If you want to work here, young man," said a personnel manager, "there are two things you should know. First, we are very keen on cleanliness. Did you wipe your feet on the mat before you came in?" – "Yes, of course, sir," replied the applicant. – "And there's another thing you should know," the manager went on, "we're very keen on honesty, too. There is no mat."

C Idioms AT WORK

TASK 1: What's the opposite?

Tim was given a *golden* hand-shake.	Tina was given a _____ handshake.
Tom has got a *steady job*.	I'm at a ____ _____ at the moment.
There are *plenty more fish* in the sea.	Good workers are _____ and _____ _____.
He dots the "i"s *and crosses the "t"s.*	He has _____ *down* ___ *the* ___.
He always gives *me a rough ride.*	He always _____ Bob *to the* _____.

TASK 2: Odd man out

Which phrase doesn't suit the sentence?

1. This job seems within my area of knowledge and interest.
   A. It seems right up my street.
   B. It's on my way.
   C. That's my line of business.

2. Let's sift through the application forms to distinguish qualified applicants from unqualified ones.
   A. separate the black cats from the white ones.
   B. separate the wheat from the chaff.
   C. separate the sheep from the goats.

3. How many salespersons have we got?
   A. Well then, let's count heads.
   B. We'd better start counting noses.
   C. Ok, let's draw numbers.

4. The boss criticised us harshly.
   A. He gave us a good shampoo.
   B. He gave us a rough ride.
   C. We were given the third degree.

5. Bad times – 300 people were given the push at a plant in Heidelberg.
   A. 300 hundred got the boot.
   B. 300 got the axe.
   C. 300 hundred got their walking cards.

Talking at cross-purposes

A businessman was interviewing a nervous young woman for a position in his company. He wanted to find out something about her personality, so he asked, "If you could have a conversation with someone living or dead, who would it be?" The girl thought about the question: "The living one," she replied.

TASK 3: Streamline your English

Replace the expressions in *italics* with one of our idioms.

1. She writes well enough, but she's *inferior* to the more serious novelists.
2. Our plans are now well advanced so I need to *fully inform* you about the project.
3. She's just joined the department – it'll take a week or two to *explain the rules to her.*
4. He's *very experienced at* programming.
5. You'll have to *become properly organized* if you want to pass the exam.
6. I was *among a small number of candidates for the job from which the successful candidate would be selected*, but I didn't get it.

TASK 4: Assonance and alliteration. It's all about sounds!

1. It's really scraping the *b*_____ of the *b*_____ *l* when you have to bring players out of retirement to make up a team.
2. The sunny intervals we were promised have been *f*_____ and *f*_____ between.
3. About 10 percent of trainees fail to *m*_____ the *g*_____.
4. You can't make a *s*_____ purse out of a *s*_____'s ear.
5. The new chairman was given a *r*_____ *r*_____ by certain members of the committee.

Time for a smile

A German business man entered a Swiss bank. He looked carefully around, went to the reception desk and whispered, "I want to invest 300,000 marks."

"You needn't whisper," said the bank clerk, "poverty is nothing to be ashamed of."

TASK 5: Magic squares – Animal idioms

Match the phrases (1, 2, 3) with the animals (A, B, C). Put the numbers in the magic squares. Columns and rows will all add up to the same number, **15**.

A. sow	D. monkeys	G. horse
B. bull	E. goose	H. birds
C. dog	F. sheep	I. fish

1. If you pay peanuts you get ★.
2. You can't teach an old ★ new tricks.
3. Plan B means killing two ★ with one stone.
4. There are plenty more ★ in the sea.

5. Let's not kill the ★ that lays the golden eggs.
6. You can't make a silk purse out of a ★'s ear.
7. You're behaving like a ★ in a china shop.
8. You can lead a ★ to water, but you can't make it drink.
9. Short-listing means separating the ★ from the goats.

A =	B =	C =
D =	E =	F =
G =	H =	I =

Time for a smile

Advertisement: Photographer setting up own business[1] needs model, as sleeping or active partner[2].

Business phrases to remember:
1 set up business: *ein eigenes Geschäft aufmachen*
2 sleeping partner: *stille(r) Teilhaber(in)*

WORK AND WORKERS
ARBEIT UND ARBEITER

We fill a large part of our lives with work. Most of us do this work against payment[1]. A few people are more concerned with the quality[2] of their work, but this seems to be an old-fashioned attitude. And when we work we are interested in promotion, we want to climb the career ladder[3]. Sometimes, however, we are not so effective in our work.

Bird's eye view

1. The way we work	*Wie wir arbeiten*
2. Efficient workers	*Tüchtige Arbeiter*
3. Up and down the career ladder	*Die Karriereleiter rauf und runter*
4. Incompetent workers	*Unfähige Arbeiter*
5. Slack periods	*Leerlauf*

Time for a smile

The personnel manager called John Doorbar into the office and said, "It hasn't escaped me[4] that every time Liverpool is playing at home you ask permission to go and visit your grandmother who's seriously ill?"

"What an incredible coincidence," exclaimed the John. "You don't think, by any chance, she's faking[5] it?"

Business phrases to remember:
1 work against payment: *gegen Bezahlung arbeiten*
2 concerned with the quality: *auf Qualität bedacht sein*
3 climb the career ladder: *die Karriereleiter erklimmen*
4 it hasn't escaped me: *es ist mir nicht entgangen*
5 fake: *simulieren*

A — A FIRST TASTE of idioms

1. The way we work – *Wie wir arbeiten*

be snowed under with work	*bis zum Hals in Arbeit stecken*
bend over backwards	*sich ein Bein ausreißen*

2. Efficient workers – *Tüchtige Arbeiter*

have something at one's fingertips	*etwas aus dem Effeff beherrschen*
know something like the back of one's hand	*etwas wie seine Westentasche kennen*
toe the line	*sich anpassen; nicht aus der Reihe tanzen; sich an die Regeln halten*

Test your memory

1. We _____ over _____ to help that boy but it was a waste of time.
2. Years of experience. He's got all the knowledge at his _____.
3. The new boss is _____ _____ with work. He's got no time at all.
4. If he doesn't _____ the _____ , he'll be fired.
5. I've worked here for ten years. I know the company like the _____ _____ my _____.

Time for a smile

The director of a toilet-paper factory was giving a review of business[1]: "Consumption of our brand[2] of toilet-paper in the past year amounted to 1.5 kilos per head." One of the workers asked, "I don't understand. Why per head?"

Business phrases to remember:
1 a review of business: *Geschäftsbericht*
2 consumption per head: *Verbrauch pro Kopf*

3. Up and down the career ladder – *Die Karriereleiter rauf und runter*

(not) fill someone's shoes	*eine Nummer zu klein für jemandes Posten sein*
jump on the bandwagon.	*sich der erfolgversprechenden Seite anschließen; Trittbrettfahrer sein*
come down in the world	*tief sinken*

Test your memory: Find the mistake and correct it

1. He's not got the talent. He'll never fill his father's hat.
2. Politicians of all parties are eager to get off on the environmental bandwagon.
3. She lost her job and then she fell down in the world.

4. Incompetent workers – *Unfähige Arbeiter*

be all fingers and thumbs	*zwei linke Hände haben*
loaf around	*herumlungern*
have one's elevenses	*eine zweite Frühstückspause machen*

Test your memory: What's the *woggle*?

1. I can't even hammer a nail in. I'm all *woggles* and thumbs.
2. Stop *woggling* around and get down to some work,
3. I'm starving. It's time to have our *woggles*.

5. Slack periods – *Leerlauf*

knock off work	*die Kelle fallen lassen*
sign on	*sich arbeitslos melden*
work to rule	*Dienst nach Vorschrift machen*

X for a/e/i/o/u: How fast can you read the idioms?

1. You *knnck xff wxrk* a bit early, don't you? It's 4 o'clock!
2. *Wxrkxng tx rxlx* is also a type of industrial action.
3. They fired me, I'll have to *sxgn xn at* the job centre.

B   The main COURSE

1. The way we work – *Wie wir arbeiten*

do the donkey work	*die mühselige Knochenarbeit machen*
work like a dog / horse	*wie ein Tier schuften; sich abrackern*
work one's fingers to the bone	*sich die Finger wund arbeiten*
be rushed / run off one's feet	*bis zum Umfallen arbeiten; kein Bein auf den Boden kriegen*
work in a shabby way	*schlampig arbeiten*
be the dog's body	*Mädchen für alles sein*
be up to one's eyes / neck in work	*bis zum Hals in Arbeit stecken; alle Hände voll zu tun haben*
after a hard day's work	*nach einem harten Arbeitstag*
be swamped with paperwork	*im Papierkrieg ertrinken*
work one's butt off (sl)	*sich abrackern*
work one's balls off for someone (sl)	*sich für jemanden zu Tode schuften*

Idioms overheard

The foreman (**F**) is talking to one of his workers (**W**):

F: You've been complaining that you *do all the donkey work.* We all have a lot to do. You should keep quiet and get on with it.

W: Well, I feel *I'm working my fingers to the bone* and it's hardly worth the pay.

F: Well, if you feel like that you'd better go. You *work in a shabby way* anyway. Good-bye.

2. Efficient workers – *Tüchtige Arbeiter*

That's my baby.	*Das ist mein Projekt / Bier.*
know what's what	*sich auskennen; wissen, wo's langgeht*
know the ins and outs of something	*etwas in- und auswendig kennen; etwas gründlich beherrschen*
know the score; know all the angles	*alle Tricks / Kniffe genau kennen*
know one's onions / stuff	*sein Geschäft verstehen*
know the ropes	*den Bogen raushaben*
learn the ropes	*sich einarbeiten*
have something at one's fingertips	*etwas aus dem Effeff beherrschen*
play one's cards right; push all the right buttons	*wissen, wie man's macht; es richtig anfassen*
get the bit between one's teeth	*sich ins Zeug legen*
knuckle down to something	*sich hinter etwas klemmen; sich in etwas hineinknien*
pull one's weight	*sich voll einsetzen; seinen Mann stehen*
kill two birds with one stone	*zwei Fliegen mit einer Klappe schlagen*
do one's level best	*sein Bestes geben*
be a feather in someone's cap	*etwas mit Stolz vorzeigen können*
toe the line	*nicht aus der Reihe tanzen; politisch linientreu sein*
take the initiative	*die Initiative ergreifen*
force the pace	*ein höllisches Tempo vorlegen*
fend for oneself	*auf eigenen Beinen stehen; auf sich allein gestellt sein*
hold / keep one's end up	*seinen Mann stehen; sich nicht unterkriegen lassen*
keep one's nose to the grindstone	*sich dahinter klemmen; schuften; am Ball bleiben*
roll one's sleeves up	*die Ärmel hochkrempeln; in die Hände spucken*
pull out all the stops	*alle Register ziehen; alles dransetzen*
work hand in hand / glove	*Hand in Hand arbeiten*

keep a stiff upper lip	*Haltung bewahren*
put one's best foot forward	*sich von der besten Seite zeigen, sein Bestes geben*
work overtime	*Überstunden machen*
be a cinch	*ein Kinderspiel sein*

Idioms overheard

The new language trainer – René (**R**)and Bob (**B**):

R: Hey, Bob, the new trainer you recommended to me really *knows the ropes.* She'*s got* all the know-how *at her fingertips.*

B: Yes, she's from New Zealand, but she'*ll* certainly *keep her end up.*

R: Well, at last I've got a trainer who's able to *take the initiative.*

3. Up and down the career ladder – *Die Karriereleiter rauf und runter*

keep one's nose clean	*sich sehr korrekt verhalten; sauber bleiben*
rise in the world	*es zu etwas bringen; seinen Weg machen*
have come a long way	*es weit gebracht haben*
come up in the world	*sich hocharbeiten*
get a room on the top floor	*ein Büro in der Chefetage bekommen*
carve out one's career	*an seiner Karriere schnitzen*
carve out a name for oneself	*sich einen Namen machen*
get ahead	*einen Vorsprung bekommen; vorankommen*
rise from the ranks	*sich von ganz unten hocharbeiten*
climb the career ladder	*die Karriereleiter erklimmen*
He's a high-flier / whiz kid.	*Er ist ein Senkrechtstarter.*
walk into a job	*eine Stelle nachgeschmissen bekommen*
follow in one's footsteps	*in jemandes Fußstapfen treten*

follow someone's lead	*jemandes Beispiel folgen; sich jemanden zum Vorbild nehmen*
keep up with the Joneses	*mit anderen gesellschaftlich gleichziehen*
get in on the act; jump on the bandwagon	*Trittbrettfahrer sein; auf einen Zug aufspringen*
be in someone's good books	*bei jemandem gut angeschrieben sein; einen Stein bei jemandem im Brett haben*
play second fiddle to someone	*bei jemandem stets nur die zweite Geige spielen*
stand on one's own two feet	*auf eigenen Beinen stehen*
jump ship	*das (sinkende) Schiff verlassen*
change sides	*das Lager / die Fronten wechseln*
fall from grace	*in Ungnade fallen*
have seen better days	*bessere Zeiten gesehen haben*

Idioms overheard

The new man – Alice (A) and Jean (J):

A: What do you think of Alex, the new man?

J: Well, he's a bit of a *high-flyer*, isn't he?

A: I'm not keen on him. I think he wants to *climb the career ladder*. If he *doesn't keep his nose clean*, he'll get a shock.

J: My, my, he's certainly not *in your good books*, is he?

Food for thought

When Columbus came to America there were no taxes, no debts, the women did all the work, and the men hunted and fished all day. How did Columbus expect to improve on a system like that?

4. Incompetent workers – *Unfähige Arbeiter*

be a millstone round the employer's neck	*ein Klotz am Bein des Arbeitgebers sein*
throw a spanner in the works	*Sand ins Getriebe streuen; einen Knüppel zwischen die Beine werfen*
break / smash something to smithereens	*etwas in tausend Stücke schlagen*
not know the first thing	*nicht die geringste Ahnung haben; nicht die Bohne wissen*
turn something upside down	*die Dinge auf den Kopf stellen*
put the cart before the horse	*das Pferd vom Schwanz aufzäumen*
bite off more than one can chew	*sich zu viel vornehmen / zumuten; sich zu viel aufladen*
make heavy weather of something	*etwas beschwerlich / mühsam finden; sich mit etwas schwer tun*
conk out	*ausfallen*
not put in an appearance	*nicht auftauchen*
work at a snail's pace	*im Schneckentempo arbeiten*
be a lazybones	*ein Faulpelz sein*
catch an employee napping / red-handed	*einen Mitarbeiter bei etwas erwischen / überraschen*
build castles in the air	*(sich) Luftschlösser bauen*
twiddle one's thumbs	*Däumchen drehen*
blow the whistle on	*verpetzen; verpfeifen*
not to lift a finger	*keinen Finger krumm machen*

Time for a smile

During the war two German spies were in a pub in London. They didn't want to be recognised as Germans so one of them ordered in English, "Two martinis, please!" – "Dry?" asked the barman. – "No," said the German, "zwei!"

Idioms overheard

Boss of Purchasing (**P**) with his deputy, John (**J**):

P: I really think that Opis isn't the right supplier for us. They just *twiddle their thumbs* when we complain about something.

J: And sometimes I think that they *don't know the first thing about* commercial vehicles.

P: Well, they accepted our order of 150 trucks. I feel *they bit off more than they could chew.*

5. Slack periods – *Leerlauf*

be off duty	*nicht im Dienst sein*
take a break	*eine Pause machen*
take time off	*sich freinehmen*
ask for time off	*um Urlaub bitten*
be on the dole	*stempeln gehen*
sign on	*sich arbeitslos melden*
have time off	*freihaben*
not do a lick of work	*keinen Handschlag tun*
down tools	*die Arbeit niederlegen*
be on a go-slow	*Bummelstreik durchführen*
go on strike	*streiken; in den Ausstand treten*
bite the hand that feeds you	*Undankbarkeit zeigen; Gutes mit Schlechtem vergelten*
(not) get one's hands dirty	*sich die Hände (nicht) schmutzig machen*

Idioms overheard

Boss (**B**) arrives at the building site, worker (**W**):

B: Jeff, look at this. You *haven't done a lick of work* since I was here this morning.

W: Oh, boss, we*'ve been taking a break.* There's not much to do anyway.

B: I'll be the judge of that. Are you all on *a go-slow*, or what? Now get your tools and back to work.

C Idioms AT WORK

TASK 1: Those nasty little words

1. He's been here for years and should know the _____ and _____ of the job by now.
2. If you want to pass that exam, you'll have to knuckle _____ .
3. The airline pulled _____ all the stops to get him there _____ time.
4. I've been swamped _____ work this year.

TASK 2: Clean up the mess

Something went wrong with the words in *italics*.

1. Already at the age of 18 Tom *varced* out his *recare*.
2. His aim was to get into the *moro* at the *pot*.
3. However, he refused to *yalp nosdec difedl* to anyone.
4. Little wonder that Tom *lefl* from *carge*.

TASK 3: Idioms with a 'c'

1. Tom is lazy bones; he usually c_ _ _ _ *out* for an hour or so after his lunch break.
2. When I asked him how the exam was, he replied "It was a c_ _ _ _!'
3. And Tom is extremely unrealistic. He's always building c_ _ _ _ _ _ in the air.
4. That is why Tom tends to *bite off more than he can* c_ _ _.
5. Now Tom is thinking of c_ _ _*ing* out a name for himself as a golf trainer.

Time for a smile

An Englishman was boasting that some of his ancestors had been in the ark with Noah. "At the time of the flood," retorted the Scot, "we, the MacGregrors, had our own boat."

TASK 4: What's the *woggle*?

Replace the *woggle*. The *woggle* can be:
vegetable, animal, person, part of the body or part of a game.

1. She's an expert tax consultant. She knows her *woggles*.
2. He made her his personal assistant. That girl plays her *woggles* right.
3. We do all the *woggle*-work and the boss takes the credit!
4. I've been working my fingers to the *woggle* to build this house and now she refuses to move in with me.
5. Don't interfere with my project. It's my *woggle*!

TASK 5: Idioms from the world of crafts

spanner	ropes
millstone	tools
grindstone	cart

1. My debts were like a _____ round my neck.
2. First things first. Don't put the _____ before the horse.
3. This is sabotage! He's always trying to throw a _____ in the works.
4. The boss promised me promotion if I keep my nose to the _____.
5. Tina is very efficient. She has been with us for only two months and has already learned the _____.
6. They heard the offer. Then they downed _____.

TASK 6: Magic squares – Body idioms

Match the phrases (1, 2, 3) with the parts of the body (A, B, C). Put the numbers in the magic squares. Columns and rows will all add up to the same number, **15**.

A. back	D. neck	G. thumbs
B. hand	E. nose	H. fingertips
C. fingers	F. feet	I. teeth

1. No golf today. I'm be up to my ★ in work.
2. Only £20! I'm working my ★ to the bone. It's really not worth my while.
3. He's a brilliant negotiator! He always has all the necessary facts at his ★.
4. We need workers who take the bit between their ★.
5. Keep your ★ to the grindstone and one day you'll get promotion.
6. He knows the Rocky Mountains like the ★ of his hand.
7. Don't bite the ★ that feeds you.
8. Tom a dentist! The boy is all fingers and ★.
9. Before Christmas shop assistants are rushed off their ★.

A =	B =	C =
D =	E =	F =
G =	H =	I =

MONEY MAKES THE WORLD GO ROUND
ALLES DREHT SICH UMS GELD

Money makes the world go round, or so they say. There are many ways of making money. You can speculate at the Stock Exchange and have luck, or lose everything, as is more often the case. But most of us have to do a day's work. Often our net salary is almost not enough to make ends meet. Money makes a slave of most of us.

Bird's eye view

1. Keeping the books — *Die Bücher führen*
2. At the Stock Exchange — *An der Börse*
3. Making a living — *Seinen Lebensunterhalt verdienen*
4. More about money — *Mehr über Geld*

Time for a smile

Pupil: "What's the difference between wages and salaries, sir?"

Teacher: "Well, if you get a wage, you get paid once a week. If you get a salary, you are paid once a month. For example, I get a salary."

Pupil: "Please, sir, where do you work?"

A — A FIRST TASTE of idioms

1. Keeping the books – *Die Bücher führen*

get a windfall	*einen, unerwarteten Gewinn bekommen*
plough money into something	*Geld in etwas stecken*
cook the books	*die Bücher frisieren; Bilanzen fälschen*

Test your memory

1. We have to _____ a lot of money into R & D to get this product ready.
2. It's difficult to earn money with a salary, but winning the lottery would _____ us a nice _____ .
3. It became clear that Mr Schneider in the accounts department was _____ the books. There was a discrepancy of DM 50,000.

2. At the Stock Exchange – *An der Börse*

easy come, easy go	*wie gewonnen, so zerronnen*
get out while the going is good	*zum richtigen Zeitpunkt aussteigen*
go the whole hog	*aufs Ganze gehen; alles riskieren*

Test your memory

1. Okay, we've won some money. Now we should get out _____ the going's _____.
2. I _____ the whole _____ and spent the lot. Now I haven't got a penny to my name .
3. We won some money, then we lost some. It's all _____ come, easy _____ .

3. Making a living – Seinen Lebensunterhalt verdienen

live in clover	*leben wie die Made im Speck*
be rolling in it	*im Geld schwimmen*
be on the breadline	*am Hungertuch nagen*
live on a shoestring	*mit sehr wenig Geld auskommen*

Test your memory

1. Five children, no husband. That family's on the _____.
2. He's the owner of a famous software company. He's _____ in it.
3. Since we won the lottery we've been _____ in _____.
4. There's no money in the budget. We'll have to do the project on a _____.

4. More about money – Mehr über Geld

have a nest egg	*etwas auf der hohen Kante haben*
go Dutch	*getrennte Rechnung machen*
pay through the nose	*tüchtig blechen für etwas*
money for old rope	*rausgeschmissenes Geld*
cost an arm and a leg	*eine Stange Geld kosten; sündhaft teuer sein*

Test your memory

1. I know you've got money problems. Let's go _____.
2. They're the only supplier, we'll have to pay through the _____ for the parts.
3. She's been saving for years. I'm sure she's got a little _____ _____ somewhere.
4. They are giving us no service. It's money for _____ _____.
5. These parts are made of copper. They'll cost us an _____ and a _____.

B The main COURSE

1. Keeping the books – *Die Bücher führen*

be in the red	*rote Zahlen schreiben*
break even	*aus den roten Zahlen kommen; eine schwarze Null vor dem Komma schreiben*
be in the black	*schwarze Zahlen schreiben*
get a windfall	*einen unverhofften Gewinn machen*
make a profit	*Gewinn / Profit machen*
chicken feed / peanuts	*kleine Fische; ein Pappenstiel*
That's chicken feed for them.	*Das zahlen die doch aus der Portokasse.*
be a cash cow for the company	*ein Goldesel für die Firma sein*
break all records	*alles in den Schatten stellen*
evade taxes	*Steuern hinterziehen*
foot the bill	*die Rechnung übernehmen*
cover one's costs	*seine Kosten decken*
hold the purse strings	*den Daumen auf der Kasse haben*
raise money for a project	*Geld für ein Projekt lockermachen*
make money hand-over-fist	*Geld scheffeln*
take a loss	*Federn lassen; Verluste hinnehmen*
cut one's losses	*in den Wind schreiben; Verluste beschränken*
stand the loss	*für den Verlust aufkommen*
get a tighter grip on the purse-strings	*den Daumen fester auf dem Geldbeutel halten*
line one's pocket(s)	*in die eigene Tasche wirtschaften, sich bereichern*

Time for a smile

My old dad said I'd never make an accountant. "There are three kinds of people in this world, son," he said. "Those who can count, and those who can't."

Idioms overheard

The financial director (**F**) discusses a line of credit with the company's bank manager (**B**):

F: So we're certainly *in the black* again at CBO and we want to expand.

B: But you had to *cut your losses* this year to achieve it. You're not exactly *making money hand over fist*, are you?

F: You're right, but now we've got a product which is going to *be a real cash cow*.

2. At the Stock exchange – *An der Börse*

A bullish market – *Haussierende Börse*

play the market	*an der Börse spekulieren*
gamble in oil shares	*mit Ölaktien spekulieren*
be safe as houses	*eine bombensichere Sache sein*
be a safe bet	*eine sichere Sache sein*
make one's pile	*seine Schäfchen ins Trockene bringen*
back a winner	*auf das richtige Pferd setzen*
make a killing	*einen Reibach machen; absahnen*
be an all-time high	*auf Höchstkurs, Rekordhoch sein*
shares sky-rocket	*die Kurse schnellen in die Höhe*
go the whole hog	*aufs Ganze gehen*
get out while the going's good	*zum richtigen Zeitpunkt aussteigen*

A bearish market – *Fallende Kurse*

it's snakes and ladders	*es ist ein ständiges Auf und Ab,*
it's swings and roundabouts; easy come, easy go	*wie gewonnen, so zerronnen*
be in free fall	*im freien Fall sein*
The bottom has fallen out.	*Der Tiefstand ist erreicht.*
back a loser	*auf das falsche Pferd setzen*
back the wrong horse	*auf das falsche Pferd setzen*
come within an inch of	*beinahe erreichen; fast ans Ziel gelangen; denkbar knapp scheitern*

touch rock-bottom	*am Ende einer Talfahrt sein; die Talsohle erreichen*
In for a penny, in for a pound.	*Wer A sagt, muss auch B sagen.*

Idioms overheard

A couple of friends, Jim (**J**) and Pete (**P**), are planning their investments:

J: So, now we've found a good company we should *go the whole hog. In for a penny, in for a pound.*

P: Careful, we might *be backing* the wrong horse.

J: Pete, you've got to trust your feelings. I've never *backed a loser* till now. Come on, we can do it. We'll *make a killing.*

Time for a smile

"Don't worry," a patient told his psychiatrist, "I'll pay every penny I owe, or my name isn't Alexander the Great!"

3. Making a living – *Den Lebensunterhalt verdienen*

The sunny side of life – *Die Sonnenseite des Lebens*

be filthy / stinking rich	*vor Geld stinken*
stink of money (sl)	*vor Geld stinken*
be in the money; be made of money	*im Geld schwimmen; keine Geldsorgen haben*
have money to burn	*Geld wie Heu haben*
be rolling in money	*Geld wie Heu haben*
rake in the money	*Geld scheffeln*
live in clover	*wie die Made im Speck leben*
live in the lap of luxury	*wie Gott in Frankreich leben*
lead / live the life of Riley / Reilley	*wie Gott in Frankreich leben*
be born with a silver spoon in one's mouth	*mit einem silbernen Löffel im Mund geboren sein*

strike it rich; hit the jackpot	*ans große Geld kommen; das große Los ziehen*
make big money	*das große Geld machen*
throw money around	*mit Geld um sich werfen*
be in pocket	*gut bei Kasse sein*
sit pretty	*ausgesorgt haben; (finanziell) gut gestellt sein*
be well off	*wohlhabend sein; gut dran sein*
make a good living	*gut verdienen*
make piles of money	*sich dumm und dämlich verdienen*
Money is no object.	*Geld spielt keine Rolle.*
throw money out of the window	*Geld aus dem Fenster werfen*
be on easy street	*keine Geldsorgen haben*
bring home the bacon	*die Brötchen verdienen*
feather one's nest; make one's pile	*seine Schäfchen ins Trockene bringen*
keep / put by / save up something for a rainy day	*einen Notgroschen zurücklegen*
put money aside	*sparen; Geld auf die hohe Kante legen*

On the seamy side of life – *Auf der Schattenseite des Lebens*

have no room to swing a cat	*kaum Platz zum Umdrehen haben*
touch someone for money	*jemanden anpumpen*
work for one's keep	*für Kost und Logis arbeiten*
earn one's keep	*seinen Lebensunterhalt verdienen*
make both ends meet	*mit seinem Geld knapp über die Runden kommen*
earn a bit of pocket money	*sich ein paar Groschen dazuverdienen*
do something on a shoestring	*etwas mit einem schmalen Portemonnaie / Budget tun*
tighten / draw in one's belt	*den Gürtel enger schnallen*
rough it	*ein spartanisches Leben führen; auf vieles verzichten*
knock / set someone back	*jemanden zurückwerfen*

be out of pocket	*mit leeren Taschen dastehen*
feel the pinch / draught	*knapp bei Kasse sein*
be hard up	*knapp bei Kasse sein*
be short of a bob or two	*keine müde Mark haben; nicht das nötige Kleingeld haben*
count every penny	*jede Mark zweimal umdrehen*
keep the wolf from the door	*sich über Wasser halten*
tide someone over	*jemandem über die Runden helfen*
dip into one's savings	*ans Eingemachte gehen*
live from hand to mouth	*von der Hand in den Mund leben*
burn a hole in someone's pocket	*ein Loch in die Kasse reißen*
drain someone dry	*jemanden (finanziell) aussaugen*
work for peanuts	*für einen Hungerlohn arbeiten*
live on a pittance	*von einem Hungerlohn leben*
just manage to scrape together enough to buy something	*seinen letzten Pfennig für etwas zusammenkratzen*
buy something on tick	*etwas auf Pump kaufen*
not have a penny to one's name	*bettelarm sein; keine müde Mark haben*
be down to one's last penny / dollar	*keinen Pfennig mehr in der Tasche haben*
not have two pennies to rub together	*keinen roten Heller haben*
be stony broke; be skint; not have a red cent [US]	*klamm sein; keinen roten Heller haben; restlos abgebrannt sein*
be poor as a church mouse	*arm wie eine Kirchenmaus sein*
be on the bread-line	*hart am Existenzminimum leben*
be up to one's eyes / eyebrows in debt	*bis über beide Ohren in Schulden stecken*
be up to the hilt in debts	*bis über die Ohren verschuldet sein*

Idioms overheard

A domestic dispute between Pete (**P**) and Tina (**T**).
Topic: How will we make ends meet?

T: Two or three years ago we were *living in the lap of luxury*. I won't say we *had money to burn*, but we *were sitting pretty*.

P: Well, we haven't exactly *been throwing money out of the window*, have we?

T: And what now? We *are living from hand to mouth*. We *have to count every penny*. And look at this house. We *haven't enough room to swing a cat*.

P: Tina, listen, let's look at it positively ...

4. More about money – *Mehr über Geld*

The sound of money – *Der Klang des Geldes*

a buck / a smacker	*ein Dollar*
lolly / bread / dough / dosh (sl)	*Knete / Kohle / Kies / Zaster*
a quid(sl)	*ein Pfund Sterling*
be worth a fortune	*ein Vermögen wert sein*
exchange money	*Geld (um)tauschen*
turn into cash	*zu Geld machen*
get one's money's worth	*etwas für sein Geld bekommen*
when I'm in the money / black again	*wenn ich wieder bei Kasse bin*
get hold of some money	*zu Geld kommen*
make a fast buck	*das schnelle Geld machen*
make some dough (sl)	*Kohle machen*

Spending money – *Geld ausgeben*

fork out money (sl)	*Geld hinblättern*
shell out; stump up (sl)	*Geld rausrücken, ausspucken*
a drop in the bucket; a grain of sand on the beach	*ein Tropfen auf dem heißen Stein*

cost the earth	*ein Vermögen kosten*
charge the earth	*ein Vermögen verlangen*
foot the bill	*die Rechnung bezahlen*
cost a pretty packet	*eine Stange Geld kosten*
blow money	*Geld verprassen / verpulvern*
cough up for something	*Geld für etwas ausspucken*
rip somebody off	*jemanden neppen*
spend one's money like it's going out of style	*mit seinem Geld um sich schmeißen*
cost an arm and a leg	*sündhaft teuer sein*
pay through the nose for something	*tüchtig bluten für etwas*
The money's down the drain.	*Das Geld ist futsch.*

(**Sayings**)

Not for love nor money.	*Nicht für Geld und gute Worte.*
All they're after is your money.	*Die sind doch nur hinter deinem Geld her.*
Hundred pounds – that's not to be sneezed at.	*Hundert Pfund – das ist nicht zu verachten.*
Money is no object.	*Geld spielt keine Rolle.*
All he (ever) thinks of is money.	*Er denkt nur ans Geld.*
Money's not everything.	*Geld allein macht nicht glücklich.*
Every little helps.	*Kleinvieh macht auch Mist.*
Look after the pennies and the pounds will look after themselves.	*Wer den Pfennig nicht ehrt, ist des Talers nicht wert.*

Idioms overheard

Two friends, Ron (**R**) and Frank (**F**), on the topic of insurances:

R: So, I'm not worth a fortune, *but every little helps.* I'm going to get a life insurance. That's *money well spent.*

F: My god, you don't want to *fork out* to an insurance company. They'll only *rip you off.*

R: Why not? It doesn't *cost the earth.* Those terminal bonuses *are not to be sneezed at.*

F: You're just as naïve as you ever were.

C   Idioms AT WORK

TASK 1:   Missing letters (they are all vowels)

1. We've already *pl _ _ gh _d* too much money into this old house.
2. Who's going to *f _ _ t* the bill for all the repairs?
3. I'm afraid we won't even be able to *c _ v _ r* the costs of the new roof.
4. We must somehow *r _ _ s _* money for the repairs. This house is worth it.

TASK 2:   Those nasty little words

1. Tom gave me a tip-off! Buy Bayer! It's ____ safe ____ houses, he said.
2. I came ____ an inch of selling my shares ____ an all-time-high.
3. You should have got ____ ____ the going was good.
4. Well, the next day the bottom had fallen ____ ____ the stock market.

TASK 3:   They have almost the same meaning

1. be up to one's eyes in debt	be up to the _____ in debts
2. not have a red cent _____	not have two _____ to together
3. just manage to scrape together enough money to make a living	make _____ ends _____

TASK 4:   At the fortune teller's

1. Will we be in the black?	No, you'll be in the _____.
2. Will we get a bullish market?	No, we'll get a _____ market.
3. Are we backing a *winner*?	No, you're backing a _____.
4. Will our shares be in free fall?	No, they'll _____-_____ again.

TASK 5: Tim, the 'Yes-man'

Tim echoes Tom using an idiom that has the same meaning as Tom's words in *italics*.

1.

Tom: Trade at the stock exchange has *dropped to a very low level*.

Tim: Yes, the bottom has _____ out of the _____.

2.

Tom: Jenny *made her pile* with investments on the New Market.

Tim: Yes, good old Jenny has _____ her nest.

3.

Tom: They also say she wrote a book which has brought an *unexpected profit*.

Tim: Yes indeed, this publication brought her a nice _____.

4.

Tom: Her brother John on the other hand is *risking a lot of money by investing in* oil shares.

Tim: Yes, he seems to be _____ _____ oil shares.

5.

Tom: John should has *already lost a fortune* at the stock exchange *and should stop it before he loses too much*.

Tim: I agree, it's high time that he _____ his *losses*.

6.

Tom: His wife and kids are already starting *to suffer from a lack of money*.

Tim: They are obviously beginning to *feel* the _____ .

TASK 6: Odd man out

Which idiom does not belong into the group? Tick it off and translate it.

1. Ron's parents are not happy. Ron has a wife, two children, and no job.
   A. We can't support you forever. It's time you *made some dough*.
   B. When are you going to *cook the books*?
   C. Get a job and *bring home the bacon*.
   Translation: _____ .

2. Ron has some bad news for Anne, his wife.

A. Impossible to get a job! It's time to *tighten our belts*.

B. I'm afraid we've *touched rock bottom*.

C. You won't like it, but we'll have *live on a shoestring*.

Translation: _____

3. Anne tells Ron to touch his grandmother for money, because the old woman

A. is on the bread-line,

B. is rolling in money,

C. is in pocket.

Translation: _____

TASK 7: | Magic squares – The animal world

Match the phrases (1, 2, 3) with the words in boxes (A, B, C). Put the numbers in the magic squares. Columns and rows will all add up to the same number, **15**.

A. cat	D. mouse	G. chicken
B. horse	E. cow	H. egg
C. nest	F. hog	I. wolf

1. Intrasoft lost 30 percent. I'm afraid you backed the wrong ★.

2. I won £45 in the lottery. But it's just ★ feed.

3. We bought 50 Ruver shares, and then decided to go the whole ★ and invest the rest of our money as well.

4. I earn enough to keep the ★ from the door.

5. The new product is our cash ★.

6. We have no room to swing a ★ but we can't afford a bigger flat.

7. He pretends to be as poor as a church ★, but we know better.

8. She married the boss's son. She's feathered her ★.

9. He made 75,000 at the stock exchange – a nice nest ★ to have.

A =	B =	C =
D =	E =	F =
G =	H =	I =

RESEARCH & DEVELOPMENT
ENTWICKLUNG & FORSCHUNG

Research and Development is a very important department in a company. They need to have the product ideas to satisfy the market. If, however, ideas don't come, this will be reflected in the quality of the product[1]. And this will mean loss of image[2] for the company.

Nevertheless, it's often difficult for R & D to get the budget they need to work efficiently[3].

Bird's eye view

1. An idea is born	*Eine Idee wird geboren*
2. Achieving a breakthrough	*Den Durchbruch schaffen*
3. Flops and failures	*Pleiten und Pannen*

Food for thought: The fitness phone

Lazy, fat teenagers are frequently the primary telephone users in a family. The inventor Kenji Kawakami has found the solution: the fitness phone. It increases fitness, turns fat into muscle and reduces phone bills[4]. The five-kilo standard model means that most calls will run under three minutes.

Business phrases to remember:
1 be reflected in the quality: *sich in der Qualität widerspiegeln*
2 loss of image for the company: *Imageverlust für die Firma*
3 work efficiently: *effektiv arbeiten*
4 reduce a bill: *eine Rechnung reduzieren*

A   A FIRST TASTE of idioms

1. An idea is born – *Eine Idee wird geboren*

rack one's brain	*sich den Kopf zermartern*
have a brainwave	*einen Geistesblitz haben*
bash one's head a against a brick wall	*gegen eine Wand anrennen*

Test your memory: What's the *woggle*?

1. We have *woggled our brains* for a solution.
2. Unless someone has a *woggle* soon we'll never solve this problem.
3. Don't bother trying to solve the problem, you're only *woggling* your *woggle* against a *woggle*.

2. Achieving a breakthrough – *Den Durchbruch schaffen*

proceed by trial and error	*nach Versuch und Irrtum vorgehen*
put to the acid test	*auf Herz und Nieren prüfen*
the greatest thing since sliced bread	*das Beste seit Erfindung der Bratkartoffel*

Test your memory:
The order of the letters has been messed up.

1. After having failed the Elk test, the new Mercedes was *put to the daic sett.*
2. We tried various methods and found the solution *by trail and rorer.*
3. The portable phone (or 'Handy' as the Germans call it) is the *greatest thing nices cisled beard.*

3. Flops and failures – *Pleiten und Pannen*

backfire on someone	*nach hinten losgehen*
come a cropper	*auf die Nase fallen*
give up the ghost	*den Geist aufgeben*

Test your memory

1. We'll _____ a real _____ if we don't prepare the product launch[1] carefully.

2. The new project has _____ on the company in a bad way.

3. My car seems to have finally _____ up the _____.

Time for a smile

Don't worry about your product

If the product kills 10 percent of the market, that still leaves you the remaining 100 percent.

If you are a big enough company, your mistakes become standards.

B　　　**The main COURSE**

1. An idea is born – *Eine Idee wird geboren*

rack one's brain	*sich den Kopf zerbrechen*
beat / bang / one's head against a stone / brick wall	*gegen eine Wand anrennen*
pick someone's brains	*jemanden aushorchen /ausquetschen; geistige Anleihen bei jemandem machen*

Business phrases to remember:
1 prepare the product launch: *die Markteinführung vorbereiten*

Whose brain child is this?	*Wer ist der geistige Vater?*
Who is the brain behind it?	*Wessen Idee ist das?*
make bricks without straw	*etwa: mit dem Bordwerkzeug aus-kommen müssen*
keep up with the times	*mit der Zeit gehen*
break (fresh) ground	*Neuland erschließen; neue Wege eröffnen*
hit on an idea	*eine gute Idee haben*
have a flash of inspiration	*einen Geistesblitz haben*
get a bright idea	*einen sehr guten Einfall haben*
have a brain wave	*einen Geistesblitz / eine tolle Idee haben*
be a stroke of genius	*ein Geniestreich sein*
find the philosopher's stone	*den Stein der Weisen finden*
hit the mark	*genau das Richtige ansprechen; ins Schwarze treffen*
spread like wildfire	*sich in Windeseile verbreiten; sich wie ein Lauffeuer verbreiten*

Idioms overheard

At Highmountain Concrete. Director Friedl (**F**) and Mr Smith (**S**), Head of Research are talking about the new prototype:

F: This concrete is as hard as iron. *Whose brainchild is it?*

S: It's mine, actually. I *picked the staff's brains* because we were in such a hurry.

F: Well, it's a great invention. You've really *hit the mark*. The market's crying out for a fast-drying concrete in high quality. Well done!

2. Achieving a breakthrough – *Den Durchbruch schaffen*

make a breakthrough	*den Durchbruch schaffen*
open up new fields	*neue Gebiete erschließen*
achieve a breakthrough	*einen Durchbruch erzielen*
proceed by trial and error	*nach Versuch und Irrtum vorgehen*

pave the way for	den Weg ebnen; die Weichen stellen für
blaze the trail / way	den Weg bereiten; Neuland betreten; Pionierarbeit leisten
be brand new	funkelnagelneu sein
lick into shape	den letzten Schliff geben
be a foolproof security system	ein todsicheres Sicherheitssystem sein
bring up-to-date	auf den neuesten Stand bringen
hit the nail on the head	den Nagel auf den Kopf treffen
hit pay dirt	Erfolg haben; auf Gold stoßen
be a fail-safe device / mechanism	ein pannensicheres System sein
be state-of-the-art	auf dem neuesten Stand der Technik sein
put to the acid test	auf Herz und Nieren prüfen
get something off the ground	etwas in Gang bringen; verwirklichen
pull something off	erfolgreich durchführen
measure up to expectations	den Erwartungen entsprechen
be up to specs	den Anforderungen entsprechen
come into use	in Gebrauch kommen; erstmals verwendet werden
go out of use	aus der Mode kommen; außer Gebrauch kommen
come up to scratch / standard	den Erwartungen entsprechen
break all records	alle Rekorde brechen; alles in den Schatten stellen
be the best / greatest thing since sliced bread	das Beste seit Erfindung der Bratkartoffel sein

Idioms overheard

At Lowvalley Photocopiers Dr Snow (**S**), Head of Research, and Director Heath (**H**) are having an argument over a component of a photocopier:

S: This technology has *gone out of use*. It was outdated years ago.

H: This technology *broke all records* in its day.

S: In its day, exactly! And its day has passed. Nowadays we need *a failsafe device* with no risks involved.

3. Flops and failures – *Pleiten und Pannen*

bark up the wrong tree	*auf dem Holzweg sein*
make a mess of something	*etwas völlig vermasseln*
gum something up	*etwas verpfuschen; Mist bauen*
back the wrong horse	*auf das falsche Pferd setzen*
Too many cooks spoil the broth.	*Zu viele Köche verderben den Brei.*
throw caution to the winds	*alle Vorsicht über Bord werfen*
get off on the wrong foot	*es falsch anpacken*
fall flat on one's face	*eine Bauchlandung machen*
cock / screw up something (sl)	*etwas versauen / verpatzen*
go to pot	*zu Bruch gehen*
go to pieces	*in die Brüche gehen*
go up in flames / smoke	*sich in Luft / nichts auflösen*
be (just) a flash in the pan	*nur ein kurzlebiger Erfolg / eine Eintagsfliege sein*
blow up in one's face	*sich als Eigentor erweisen*
go haywire	*verrückt spielen; schief gehen*
be Murphy's / sod's law (sl)	*das ungeschriebene Gesetz, wonach alles schief gehen wird, was schief gehen kann*
blow one's chance	*seine Chance verspielen*
go down the drain / tube	*den Bach runtergehen; für die Katz sein*
hit-and-miss work	*Arbeit aufs Geratewohl, auf gut Glück*
be on the blink	*kaputt sein; nicht funktionieren*
draw a blank	*kein Glück haben; eine Niete ziehen*
go pear-shaped (sl)	*schief gehen; sich ins Gegenteil kehren*
make a cock-up (sl)	*etwas vermasseln, in den Sand setzen*
be up the spout	*im Eimer sein*
go back to the drawing board.	*wieder ganz von vorn anfangen müssen*
be / go back to square one	*wieder da sein, wo man angefangen hat*
miss the boat	*den Anschluss / die Entwicklung verpassen*

come a cropper	*auf die Nase fallen*
be a complete flop	*ein Schuss in den Ofen sein*
be a washout	*ein Versager sein*
be a dead loss / turkey	*ein totaler Reinfall / hoffnungsloser Fall sein*
end up with an egg on one's face	*sich lächerlich machen; sich blamieren*
be the scapegoat / the whipping-boy	*der Sündenbock / Prügelknabe sein*
It's no use crying over spilt milk.	*Geschehen ist geschehen. Hin ist hin.*

Idioms overheard

George (**G**) and Tom (**T**), employees at a small mechanical engineering company

G: I'm worried about the future of our company. We haven't any new ideas, any patents. Without technology the company will *be up the spout*.

T: I agree with you. I'm beginning to think I *backed the wrong horse* when I came here.

G: Our products aren't state-of-the-art. In my opinion *it's all hit-and-miss* with us. And that's not how I want my future.

C   Idioms AT WORK

TASK 1:   Let's go *woggling* again

The R & D department leader (**L**) has a difficult talk with a new employee (**E**):

L: Somehow your work seems to have *woggled* off on the wrong *woggle*. The results aren't satisfactory.

E: I know. I've drawn a *woggle* with almost every project. I feel like I'm having a rough ride in my new job.

TASK 2: Get your idioms right

The Chief Engineer (**E**) is in discussion with the Finance Director (**F**): Something went wrong here in *italics*. Can you repair the damage?

E: We got a chance to *nope* up new *fidles*, and it means our copiers will remain *taste* of the *rat*.

F: That might well be, but we're getting beyond our budget.

E: But you have to have vision. I feel I'm *tebaing* my head against a *cbrki awll*. Let me try to explain ...

TASK 3: Fill in the blanks

Salesman (**S**) explains some features to a customer (**C**):

S: And our copier produces three thousand copies an hour. That
b_____ all r_____.

C: Very good, but the _____ test is whether the copies are in usable quality.

S: The technology is _____ new and this guarantees excellent print quality.

C: I must say that your last product caused a lot of problems. We had to lick the machine into _____.

S: Of course, it's no good _____over _____ milk.

TASK 4: Tom, the 'Yes-man'

Complete the consonants in the idioms.

1

Tim: Haven't we been *trying hard to think* of new products and procedures?

Tom: Yes, we've been _ a _ _ ing our _ _ ai _ _ trying to find something.

2

Tim: But how on earth can we do *research without the necessary material, money and information*?

Tom: You're right, you can't make _ _ i_ _ _ without _ _ _ a _.

3

Tim: That is why work in this department is *not done in a careful or planned way and is not likely to be effective or successful.*

Tom: Yes, it's all _ i _-a _ _ -_ i _ _ experimentation.
                              4

Tim: And when something goes down the spout we are supposed to accept the blame.

Tom: Yes, they expect us to _ a _ e the _ a _.
                              5

Tim: It's high time somebody had a *clever idea*.

Tom: Yes, what we need is a _ _ ai _ _a _ e .

TASK 5: | **Magic squares**

Match the phrases (1, 2, 3) with the words in the box (A, B, C). Put the numbers in the magic squares. Columns and rows will all add up to the same number, **15**.

A. track	D. broth	G. horse
B. tree	E. milk	H. wrong
C. bread	F. egg	I. foot

1. He was left with ★ all over his face when his forecast was proved wrong.
2. We haven't found a cure yet, but I'm sure we're on the right ★.
3. The experiment went disastrously ★.
4. The anti-fat pill is a loser. We've backed the wrong ★?
5. It's no use crying over spilt ★.
6. Vagira is the best thing since sliced ★.
7. If you think that, you're barking up the wrong ★ altogether.
8. I think we got off on the wrong ★ with the launch of Vigira 2.
9. Too many cooks spoil the ★.

A =	B =	C =
D =	E =	F =
G =	H =	I =

BUYING AND SELLING
KAUFEN UND VERKAUFEN

Companies buy as cheaply as possible and sell to make a maximum profit. However, the whole situation is complicated by rules, regulations, discounts and time-lines. As a result we have specialist departments in companies concentrating on issues of how to buy and sell as economically as possible.

Bird's eye view

1. Discussing the price	*Über den Preis sprechen*
2. Buying	*Kaufen*
3. Selling	*Verkaufen*
4. Phrases for salesmen	*Ausdrücke für Verkäufer*
5. Customer Service	*Kundendienst*

Let's start with a smile

The USP – the unique selling proposition:
A door-to-door salesman knocked at the door of a typical suburban house in Wimbledon.
"Good morning," he said. "Would you care to buy a copy of 'Five Hundred Excuses To Give Your Wife For Staying Out Late'?"
"Why on earth would I want a book like that?" said the lady.
"Because," replied the salesman, "I sold a copy to your husband at his office this morning."

A — A FIRST TASTE of idioms

1. Discussing the price – *Über den Preis sprechen*

dip into one's pocket	*(tief) in die eigene Tasche greifen*
cost an arm and a leg	*ein Vermögen kosten*
It's a snip / bargain.	*Das ist ein Schnäppchen.*

Test your memory

1. The Robinson Club? You'll have to _____ *into* your _____ if you want to go there.
2. We're not going there again. It *cost* me an _____ and a _____.
3. You must admit that I'm offering you a bargain. That car's *a* _____ at only $5000!

2. Buying – *Kaufen*

buy a pig in a poke	*die Katze im Sack kaufen*
get it for next to nothing	*etwas für 'nen Appel und 'n Ei bekommen*
pay up front	*im Voraus / bar bezahlen*

Test your memory: What's the *woggle*?

1. I don't accept cheques. You have to *pay up woggle* if you want to buy from me.
2. My laptop was a really good bargain. I *got it for woggle to nothing.*
3. If you don't do some research on it you'll be *buying a pig in a woggle.*

3. Selling – *Verkaufen*

sell at a dumping price	*unter Selbstkosten / zu einem Schleuderpreis verkaufen*
sell one's own grandmother	*seine eigene Großmutter verkaufen*
suit someone down to the ground	*genau das Richtige für jemanden sein*

Test your memory

1. You can't trust him. He'd *sell* his _____ _____.
2. Our competitors are selling goods ____ a _____ *price*. We haven't got a chance.
3. This house is just what I want. It suits me _____ to the _____.

How to canvass[1] effectively

One door-to-door salesman does very well by using the opening line: "Can I interest you in something your neighbour said you couldn't possibly afford?"

Business phrase to remember:
1 canvass: *Kundenbesuche machen*

B   The main COURSE

1. Discussing the price – *Über den Preis sprechen*

cost an arm and a leg	*ein Vermögen kosten*
cost a pretty penny	*ein schönes Stück Geld kosten*
cost a packet	*eine Stange Geld kosten*
jack up prices	*Preise erhöhen*
hike up the rent	*Miete erhöhen / anheben*
be a smack in the face	*ein Schlag ins Gesicht sein*
Prices go through the roof.	*Preise steigen schwindelerregend.*
pay through the nose	*bluten / blechen müssen*
dip into one's pocket	*(tief) in die eigene Tasche greifen*
offer the chance of a lifetime	*eine einmalige Chance bieten*
come halfway on the price	*beim Preis auf halbem Wege entgegen-* *kommen*
cut prices	*mit den Preisen runtergehen*
It's a snip / bargain.	*Das ist ein Schnäppchen.*
It's a bit steep.	*Das ist ganz schön happig / gesalzen.*

Idioms overheard

Mr Stelzer (**S**), boss of Purchasing Services, has a discussion with a supplier, Mr Ling (**L**):

S: And so as I was saying, your prices *are going through the roof*. We can't accept this situation.

L: We've got our costs, too. Our translators are getting more and more expensive. They *are costing us a packet*.

S: Nevertheless, we have to find a compromise. It's simply too expensive.

2. Buying – *Kaufen*

It's going for a song.	*Es ist für einen Spottpreis zu haben.*
get (it) for next to nothing	*fast umsonst bekommen*
be worth one's money	*sein Geld wert sein*
get one's money's worth	*etwas für sein Geld bekommen*
get value for money	*preiswert sein; reell bedient werden*
offer a knock-down / giveaway / throwaway price	*zum Einführungs- / Schleuderpreis anbieten*
jump at an offer	*bei einem Angebot schnell zugreifen*
fall for it	*darauf hereinfallen*
buy a pig in a poke	*die Katze im Sack kaufen*
buy a white elephant	*ein Groschengrab / einen lästigen, kostspieligen Besitz erwerben*
make a bad buy	*sich verkaufen; einen schlechten Kauf machen*
fill the bill	*seine Aufgabe / seinen Zweck erfüllen*
suit someone down to the ground	*genau das Richtige für jemanden sein*
It suits me to a T.	*Das ist haargenau das Richtige für mich.*
pull the wool over someone's eyes	*jemanden hinters Licht führen*
rip someone off	*jemanden übers Ohr hauen*
pay up front	*bar und im Voraus zahlen*
pay cash on the nail	*das Geld bar auf den Tisch des Hauses blättern*
buy / get something on tick	*etwas auf Pump kaufen*
buy (pay) in dribs and drabs	*auf Raten / kleckerweise kaufen*
buy on HP (hire purchase)	*auf Raten kaufen*
That's a fraud.	*Das ist ja Betrug.*
Don't look a gift horse in the mouth.	*Einem geschenkten Gaul schaut man nicht ins Maul.*

Idioms overheard

At the second-hand car showrooms. Customer (**C**) and salesman (**S**):

S: And this marvellous Ford here will certainly *fill the bill*. Just look! It's only got 40,000 km on the clock[1].

C: Hey, I*'m not falling for that*.

S: Hey man! This car's *real value for money*. You must be joking.

C: Okay, okay. Oh, by the way, can I buy this car *on the drip*?

S: Come on, I wasn't born yesterday.

3. Selling – *Verkaufen*

land an order	*einen Auftrag ergattern / an Land ziehen*
change hands	*den Besitzer wechseln*
meet someone's needs	*jemandes Bedürfnisse befriedigen*
meet / cover the demand	*den Bedarf decken*
push / boost sales	*den Verkauf ankurbeln*
scrape the bottom of the barrel	*den letzten schäbigen Rest zusammenkratzen*
test the hard sell	*aggressive Verkaufsstrategien erproben*
sell one's own grandmother	*sogar seine eigene Großmutter verkaufen*
a salesman as tough as leather	*ein zäher, abgebrühter Verkäufer*
practise soft sell	*weiche Verkaufsstrategie verfolgen*
sell under the counter	*unter der Hand / dem Ladentisch verkaufen*
throw dust in someone's eyes	*jemandem Sand in die Augen streuen*
talk someone into buying something	*jemandem etwas aufschwatzen*
railroad someone into buying something	*jemandem etwas aufdrängen*
fob something off on someone	*jemandem etwas andrehen*
fleece someone	*jemanden ausnehmen*
sell someone short	*jemanden übers Ohr hauen*

Business phrase to remember:
1 40,000 km on the clock: *40.000 km auf dem Tacho*

take someone for a ride	*jemanden reinlegen*
sell someone a pup	*jemandem Ramsch andrehen*
be as common as muck (sl)	*Dutzendware / Schund sein*
sell someone a shelf-warmer	*jemandem einen Ladenhüter verkaufen*
get stuck with the goods	*auf der Ware sitzen bleiben*
sell at a loss	*mit Verlust verkaufen*
get / gain the edge over one's competitors	*die Konkurrenz überflügeln*
sell at a dumping price	*zu einem Schleuderpreis / unter Selbstkosten verkaufen*
fetch a good price	*einen guten Preis erzielen*
be a good seller	*sich gut verkaufen*
be a money spinner	*ein Renner sein*
be a cash-cow	*der Goldesel sein*
sell like hot cakes	*weggehen wie warme Semmeln*
Sales are rocketing.	*Der Absatz schnellt in die Höhe.*
Don't count your chickens before they're hatched.	*Verkaufe das Fell nicht, bevor du den Bären erlegt hast.*

Idioms overheard

Two partners discuss a room which one of them has rented for the company. John (J) and Tom (T):

J: What the hell have you been doing? Look at this room!

T: Oh, come on! It'll *meet our needs* perfectly.

J: Rubbish! You've really *scraped the bottom of the barrel* with this. What shabby decor! We can't bring a customer here. Someone really *fobbed that off on you.*

T: We need more space. And look at the location. We'll *gain a serious edge over our competitors.*

4. Phrases for salesmen – *Ausdrücke für Verkäufer*

fit like a glove	*wie angegossen sitzen*
First come, first served.	*Wer zuerst kommt, mahlt zuerst.*
be tailor-made	*maßgeschneidert sein*
be someone's bread-and-butter	*jemandes täglich Brot / Existenzgrundlage sein*
two for the price of one	*zwei zum Preis von eins*
do oneself a good turn	*sich was Gutes tun*
That's the beauty of it!	*Das ist das Schöne daran!*

5. Customer Service – *Kundendienst*

The customer is king.	*Der Kunde ist König.*
roll out the red carpet	*den roten Teppich ausrollen*
give someone a fair / square deal	*mit jemandem ehrliche Geschäfte machen*
gift-wrap something	*etwas als Geschenk einpacken*
lose one's cool	*auf die Palme gehen*
cool down	*von der Palme herunterkommen*
treat someone like dirt	*jemanden wie den letzten Dreck behandeln*
butter someone up	*jemandem Honig um den Bart schmieren / ihn einseifen*
It's a rip-off!	*Das ist Wucher!*
All that glitters is not gold.	*Es ist nicht alles Gold, was glänzt.*

Idioms overheard

In the after-sales department of a famous store. Angry customer (**C**), department leader (**L**):

C: Don't try to *butter me up*! I've seen through you. I bought this vacuum cleaner and it blows instead of sucking. *It's a rip-off*!

L: Yes, I quite agree with you, but fair's fair. There is a problem, but we can solve it together.

C: I hope so. Okay, what's your suggestion?

C Idioms AT WORK

TASK 1: Odd man out

Which idiom does **not** fit the context? Translate the odd man.

1. Don't trust this salesman. He tries to ...
   A. fleece you.
   B. short sell you.
   C. gift-wrap you.
   Translate:_____

2. This vase is not antique and much too expensive.
   A. It's a snip.
   B. It's a bit steep.
   C. That's a forgery.
   Translate:_____

3. Real antiques are far and few between and ...
   A. they cost an arm and a leg.
   B. they cost next to nothing.
   C. they cost a packet.
   Translate:_____

4. Bayer took the drug Lipobay off the market. It used to be their
   A. cash cow.
   B. money spinner.
   C. shelf-warmer.
   Translate:_____

TASK 2: Make up your mind

Which idiom fits the context best?

1. The salesman said the car was in good condition, and I was foolish
   enough to (**A**) *fall for it* / (**B**) *jump at it*.
2. You're wrong. The car is a chance of a lifetime. If I'd been offered it,
   I'd have (**A**) *fallen for it* / (**B**) *jumped at it*.

3. The salesman didn't accept my card. I had to (A) *pay up front* / (B) *pay in dribs and drabs*.
4. She didn't pay me all at once but (A) *on tick* / (B) *in dribs and drabs*.
5. Tourists complain of being (A) *ripped off* / (B) *railroaded* by local taxi-drivers.

TASK 3: Find the opposite

Harry Potter books are *good sellers*.	The self-help book 'All I know about women' is a _____.
Cigarettes must be paid *up front*.	Cars may be bought on _____ _____.
Tourists hope to *be given a square deal*.	In some countries, however, they *are* often _____ off.
Some tourists *lose their cool* when they are fleeced.	But they quickly _____ *down* again over a good glass of wine.

Time for a a smile

Selling is the most exciting thing you can do with your clothes on.
John Fenton

TASK 4: Tim, the 'Yes-man'

Complete Tim's idiomatic echo.

1.

Tom: Tina wants to buy that pent house from the White Elephant Agency. I'm afraid the prices of property have *risen very rapidly*.

Tim: Yes, I know. Property prices have gone _____ the _____.

2.

Tom: She thinks that pent house is an *exceptional opportunity*.

Tim: Yes, she thinks it's the _____ of a _____.

3.

Tom: She'll pay *far too much money* for a house in that neighbourhood.

Tim: Yes, she'll pay _____ the _____ for a house in that area.

4.

Tom: And the repairs alone will already *cost a large sum of money.*

Tim: The repairs will cost an _____ and a _____.

5.

Tom: I suppose her fiancé *forced her* to buy it.

Tim: So do I. Her fiancé must have _____ her into buying it.

6.

Tom: Poor Tina! The White Elephant Agency will sell her *a house that is worth much less than the price she'll pay for the repairs.*

Tim: Yes, they will sell her a _____.

A good bargain

The following conversation took place at a Rolls Royce car showroom:

"If I buy one of these cars on credit," asked a customer, "how long will I have to pay for it?"

"It depends on how much you can pay each month," replied the salesman.

The man paused, "25 pounds, more or less."

"Well then," said the salesman laughing, "it will take you about a hundred years."

"Excellent. Let's sign the contract."

TASK 5: Magic squares – Animals and textiles

Match the phrases (1, 2, 3) with the words in the box (A, B, C). Put the numbers in the magic squares. Columns and rows will all add up to the same number, **15**.

A. chickens	D. pocket	G. horse
B. carpet	E. pig	H. glove
C. cash-cows	F. elephant	I. wool

1. At the Ritz they roll out the red ★ for any customer. Even for you.
2. Don't look a gift ★ in the mouth.
3. The new office block has become an expensive white ★.
4. A real van Gogh! Don't try to pull the ★ over my eyes.
5. Buying paintings on the Internet is buying a ★ in a poke.
6. Don't count your ★ before they're hatched.
7. To marry his daughter off to Ralph he is ready to dip into his ★.
8. Lipobay used to be one of Bayer's ★.
9. I don't like this hat. – But it fits you like a ★. – Rubbish! It should fit me like a hat.

A =	B =	C =
D =	E =	F =
G =	H =	I =

Food for thought

Never simply say: "Sorry, we don't have what you are looking for."
Always say: "Too bad, I just sold the last one today."
Robert Skole

IDIOMS FOR MEETINGS
IDIOMS FÜR BESPRECHUNGEN

Meetings can be very difficult and unproductive. The well-organised meeting needs a chairperson who moves things along, but at the same time supports the weaker participants. It could also be that the participant is nervous and not a good group member. It's the task of the chairperson to run the meeting efficiently and on schedule[1].

Bird's eye view

1. Opening the meeting	*Die Besprechung eröffnen*
2. Maintaining discipline	*Disziplin aufrechterhalten*
3. Evaluating arguments	*Argumente bewerten*
4. The typical participant	*Der typische Teilnehmer*
5. Closing the meeting	*Die Besprechung beenden*

Advice from the expert

1. Never arrive on time: this stamps you as a beginner[2].
2. Don't say anything until the meeting is half over: this stamps you as wise.
3. Be as vague as possible: this avoids irritating the others.
4. Be the first to move for adjournment[3]: this will make you popular – it's what everyone is waiting for.
5. When in doubt, suggest a subcommittee be appointed[4].
   Harry Chapmas

Business phrases to remember:
1 run a meeting on schedule: *eine Besprechung nach Zeitplan leiten*
2 stamp someone as a beginner: *jemanden als Anfänger abstempeln*
3 move for adjournment: *Vertagung beantragen*
4 suggest a subcommittee be appointed: *vorschlagen, man möge eine Unterkommission einrichten*

A — A FIRST TASTE of idioms

1. Opening the meeting – *Die Besprechung eröffnen*

kick the meeting off	*mit der Besprechung beginnen*
keep the minutes	*das Protokoll führen*

2. Maintaining discipline – *Disziplin aufrechterhalten*

(not) get side-tracked	*(nicht) vom Thema abkommen*
(not) get a word in edgeways	*(nicht) zu Wort kommen*
cut someone off	*jemanden unterbrechen*

Test your memory: What's the *woggle*?

1. Gentlemen, I want to *woggle* the meeting off exactly on time, so if you're ready ...
2. John, since you are the most accurate person here I'd like you to *woggle* the minutes.
3. Let's not get *side-woggled*. This point has nothing to do with the present issue.
4. He's always talking. I can't get a word in *woggleways*.
5. David, please don't *woggle* Tim off like that. He has every right to speak.

3. Evaluating arguments – *Argumente bewerten*

hold water	*hieb- und stichfest sein*
pick holes in an argument	*ein Argument zerpflücken*

4. The typical participant – *Der typische Teilnehmer*

hang on someone's every word	*an jemandes Lippen hängen*
be all at sea	*völlig verloren sein; im Dunkeln tappen*
drag one's feet	*langsam tun; etwas hinauszögern*

Test your memory

Nouns have slipped out of place. Where do they belong?

1. I want to sell the house, but my husband is *dragging his sea.*
2. She worships him. She *hangs on his every holes.*
3. We have to be more professional. Our advertising is *all at water.*
4. You haven't done your homework. They will *pick feet* in your arguments from top to bottom.
5. That's illogical. Your idea doesn't *hold word.*

5. Closing the meeting – *Die Besprechung beenden*

get something over and done with	*etwas hinter sich bringen*
wind up a meeting	*eine Besprechung abschließen*
come to a dead end	*in eine Sackgasse geraten*

Test your memory

1. We might as well stop. Unfortunately we've come to a _____ _____ with this topic.
2. That conference was lousy. I'm happy it's _____ and _____ with.
3. It's getting late. I guess it's time to _____ _____ the meeting.

Time for a smile

The managing director of a big company was well-known for his dominating way of handling meetings[1]. At the end of a meeting he used to look round and say:

"Let's have a vote[2] and call it a day[3]. All those who are against my suggestions raise their hands and say 'I resign'."

Business phrases to remember: 1 handle meetings: *Besprechungen leiten*
2 have a vote: *eine Abstimmung durchführen* · 3 Let's call it a day: *Feierabend für heute!*

B   The main COURSE

1. Opening the meeting – *Die Besprechung eröffnen*

call a meeting	*eine Sitzung einberufen*
take the chair	*den Vorsitz übernehmen*
declare the meeting open	*die Besprechung für eröffnet erklären*
Let's begin at the beginning.	*Beginnen wir mit dem Anfang.*
take the minutes as read	*das Protokoll billigen, als ange-nommen betrachten*
keep the minutes	*das Protokoll führen*
narrow the agenda down	*die Tagesordnung einschränken*
kick off with	*mit etwas anfangen / loslegen*
first things first	*das Wichtigste zuerst*
for openers / starters	*als Erstes; als Auftakt*
be held up by some act of God	*durch höhere Gewalt verhindert sein*
have to cover a lot of ground	*vieles zu besprechen haben*
be off the record	*inoffiziell / nicht für das Protokoll bestimmt sein*
get down to business	*sich an die Arbeit machen*
get down to brass tacks	*Nägel mit Köpfen machen*
Let the meeting roll.	*Beginnen wir die Besprechung.*

Idioms overheard

At the meeting. René (**R**), Ortrud (**O**):

R: So, *I'll take the chair* and as we're all short of time I'll try to *narrow the agenda down.*

O: Well, *for starters* I'd like to raise the question[1] of money. *Off the record*, we're going downhill rapidly.

R: The voice of doom[2] speaks again!

Business phrases to remember:
1 raise a question: *eine Frage aufwerfen*
2 the voice of doom: *die Stimme des Verhängnisses / Schicksals*

2. Maintaining discipline – *Disziplin aufrechterhalten*

Mr X, the floor is yours.	*Mr. X, Sie haben das Wort.*
It is my say / turn now!	*Jetzt rede ich!*
get / give the green light	*grünes Licht bekommen / geben*
keep the ball rolling	*die Diskussion in Gang halten*
face the problems	*sich den Problemen stellen*
take first place	*oberste Priorität haben*
cut somebody short	*jemandem ins Wort fallen*
cut something short	*etwas abkürzen; plötzlich beenden*
speak out of turn	*sich im Ton vergreifen*
be / talk at cross-purposes	*aneinander vorbeireden*
call to order	*zur Ordnung rufen*
be out of order	*danebenliegen*
get the discussion under way	*die Diskussion in Gang bringen*
come to the point	*zur Sache kommen*
make a point; make one's point	*etwas betonen*
come back down to earth	*wieder auf dem Teppich / den Boden der Tatsachen kommen*
go back to basics	*sich auf das Wesentliche besinnen*
talk turkey	*Klartext reden*
call someone's bluff	*jemanden zwingen, Farbe zu bekennen; jemanden beim Wort nehmen*
get to the bottom of	*einer Sache auf den Grund gehen*
raise a question / problem	*eine Frage zur Sprache bringen; ein Problem ansprechen*
get a second opinion	*eine zweite Meinung einholen*
go round in circles	*sich im Kreis drehen*
There's more than one way to skin a cat.	*Es gibt mehrere Wege, die zum Ziel führen.*

93

Idioms overheard

The department meeting at a photocopier company.
Department leader(**D**), project leader (**P**):

P: *Talking turkey* I'd say this project is in real trouble.

D: I *gave you the green light* to design a mini-copier two years ago. And it seems to me you've all been *going around in circles* ever since.

P: Well, I can't agree. If I could just *make my point*, it's the shortage of qualified staff[1].

D: Oh, let's not *get side-tracked* ...

3. Evaluating arguments – *Argumente bewerten*

be the crux of the matter	*der springende Punkt / das eigentliche Problem sein*
ring true	*wahr klingen*
hit the nail on the head	*den Nagel auf den Kopf treffen; richtig liegen*
a watertight argument	*ein hieb- und stichfestes Argument*
That's not my cup of tea.	*Das ist nicht mein Fall.*
That's a different kettle of fish	*Das ist eine andere Geschichte.*
It's not as simple as that.	*Es ist nicht so einfach, wie es aussieht.*
It's old hat.	*Das ist kalter Kaffee / ein alter Hut.*
be a far cry from something	*meilenweit entfernt sein von*
be off the mark / target	*an der Sache vorbeigehen*
That argument won't wash with me.	*Das Argument ist nicht stichhaltig / zieht bei mir nicht.*
be beside the point	*nicht zur Sache gehören*
cut both / two ways	*zweischneidig sein*
be full of holes	*wackelig / auf tönernen Füßen stehen*

Business phrase to remember:
1 shortage of qualified staff: *Mangel an qualifizierten Arbeitskräften*

Idioms overheard

Strategic meeting between two partners, Dick (**D**) and Jim (**J**):

J: So, I feel it's really time we set up another branch. That's *the crux of the matter.*

D: I've read your proposal, Jim, but I think it's *full of holes.* An office in a big town. *That's a different kettle of fish.* Think of the costs.

J: *That's old hat!* Think of the chances, the market.

Advice from the expert

If you want to kill an idea in the world,
get a meeting working on it.
Charles F. Kettering

---

4. The typical participant – *Der typische Teilnehmer*

1. The well prepared participants

know every trick in the book	*mit allen Wassern gewaschen sein*
be in the picture	*im Bilde sein*
prick up one's ears	*seine Ohren spitzen*
be all ears	*ganz Ohr sein*
know what's what	*wissen, was Sache ist*
see which way the cat jumps	*sehen, wohin der Hase läuft*
have the figures at one's fingertips	*die Zahlen parat haben*
be in the swim of things	*auf dem Laufenden sein*

2. The bad participants

be a know-all	*ein Besserwisser sein*
be bored to death	*tödlich gelangweilt sein*
have tunnel vision	*einen beschränkten Horizont haben*
be absent-minded	*geistesabwesend sein*
He hasn't got the foggiest idea.	*Er hat keinen (blassen) Schimmer.*

not know the first thing about	*keine Ahnung haben von*
put in one's (own) two bits	*seinen Senf dazugeben*
be a jack-of-all-trades	*ein Hansdampf in allen Gassen sein*
jump to conclusions	*voreilige Schlüsse ziehen*
talk the hind legs off a donkey	*jemandem ein Ohr / Bein ablabern*
flog a topic to death	*ein Thema zu Tode reiten*
go round with blinkers	*Scheuklappen vor den Augen haben*
see how the land lies	*die Lage peilen; das Terrain sondieren*
sit on the fence	*sich abwartend verhalten*
grope in the dark	*im Dunkeln tappen*

Idioms overheard

Discussion about potential cooperation with another company. Ron (**R**), the managing director and Bob (**B**), a shareholder:

R: I don't feel that Unlingua would play fair with us. They *know every trick in the book* in this game.

B: But they *haven't got the foggiest idea* about quality seminars, have they?

R: That's right and that's our advantage. *We're into* seminars in a big way. But Unlingua won't cooperate. They *sit on the fence* until they see *how the land lies*.

Time for a smile

The boss was addressing a meeting of the firm's senior executives and sales staff . "Now, when my son starts to work here tomorrow," he said, "I want you to treat him just as you would treat any other employee who was going to take over the company in two year's time."

5. Closing the meeting – *Die Besprechung beenden*

come down on one side of the fence or the other	*sich für die eine oder andere Seite entscheiden*
ask for a show of hands	*um Handzeichen bitten*
come to a standstill	*zum Stillstand kommen*
reach deadlock; be at a dead end	*in eine Sackgasse geraten*
break the deadlock	*(Gespräche) wieder in Gang bringen*
have the casting vote	*die ausschlaggebende Stimme haben*
carry a motion by five votes to four	*einen Antrag mit fünf zu vier Stimmen annehmen*
draw a meeting to an end / close	*eine Besprechung zum Abschluss bringen*
call it a day	*Feierabend / Schluss machen*
be at the end of the road	*am Ende angelangt sein*
pull the plug on something	*etwas beenden*
ring down the curtain on something	*etwas beenden*
wrap something up	*etwas beenden / abschließen*
break off something	*etwas abbrechen*
throw in the towel	*das Handtuch werfen*
the bottom line is ...	*Kurz und gut ..., das Fazit ist ...*
All in all that's it.	*Fertig! Erledigt! Das war's.*

Idioms overheard

Ron (**R**) and Soom (**S**) discuss books:

R: So, *the bottom line* is that I'm willing to take 400 books off your hands[1] if you grant me a 50 percent discount for quantity[2].

M: Okay, okay, you mention this every time we meet. I guess it's time to *throw in the towel*. You can have the books. Unless you two *have any other business*, I'd like to *ring down the curtain on this meeting*.

R: Okay, good idea, let's *call it quits*. Off to the restaurant!

....

Business phrases to remember:
1 take something off someone's hands: *jemandem etwas abnehmen*
2 grant discount for quantity: *einen Mengenrabatt gewähren*

C Idioms AT WORK

TASK 1: Say it with an idiom

1. limit the number of topics	_____ the agenda _____
2. make notes for the meeting	_____ the _____
3. give the right to speak	give the _____ to someone
4. say something unofficially which should not appear in the minutes	speak _____ the _____

TASK 2: Tom, the chairman, and Tim, the 'Yes-man'

1

Tom: Shall I *take the chair*?

Tim: Yes, I think you should _____ *the meeting.*

2

Tom: Then let's *kick the meeting off.*

Tim: Okay, let the meeting _____.

3

Tom: So let's get *down to business.*

Tim: Okay, let's get *down to* _____ _____.

4

Tom: We've got to discuss the budget *for starters.*

Tim: Yes, let's talk about the budget *for* _____.

5

Tom: Well, I think we've *talked about a lot of problems.*

Tim: Yes, we've *covered a lot of* _____.

6

Tom: That just about *wraps it up* for today, doesn't it?

Tim: Yes, let's _____ *it a day.*

TASK 3: Which idiom suits the context best?

1. Pete has been talking for hours boring everybody.
   A. He can talk the hind legs off a donkey.
   B. He is out in the swim.
   C. He always speaks off the record.

2. The committee is considering the proposal and we're waiting to see
   A. which side will be at the end of the road.
   B. who will sit on the fence.
   C. which side of the fence it comes down on.

3. They have failed to decide between courses of action, because they are afraid to offend the directors.
   A. So they have been flogging the topic to death.
   B. That's why they're still groping in the dark.
   C. They are sitting on the fence.

4. Although the director has retired, he tries to be up to date.
   A. He is always held up by some act of God.
   B. He reads all the minutes and that keeps him in the swim.
   C. That is the reason why he's all at sea.

5. We've covered all the topics so let's
   A. take the minutes as read.
   B. wind the meeting up.
   C. drag our feet a bit.

Time for a smile

The managing director called a meeting because the company was in serious financial trouble. The secretary came in, tiptoed up to the director and whispered into his ear, "The accountant wants to have a word with you, sir. It's urgent."

"Not now!" replied the director angrily. "Can't you see that we're in the middle of an important meeting?"

"But he is phoning from the Bahamas, sir."

TASK 4: Letter mix-up

We've mixed the letters of some words. Can you find and correct them?

1. Contributing to the success of a meeting is not as *mipsle* as that.
2. If you're out of luck the chairperson will ask you to *peek* the *tumines*.
3. Most of the time participants *lakt* at cross *peprusos*.
4. If the participants speak all at the same time the chairperson will *lacl* them to *roder*.
5. And if you speak out of *runt* the chairperson will lure you out of *order*.

TASK 5: Odd man out

Which phrase does not fit the context?

1. Your argument seems true enough to be believed.
   A. It's as clear as water.
   B. It's watertight.
   C. It holds water.

2. Your suggestion is double-edged.
   A. It cuts both ways.
   B. It's far and few between.
   C. It might have two opposite effects.

2. We're talking about losses, not about losers. Your argument is
   A. is beside the point.
   B. is off mark.
   C. is old hat.

4. I'm afraid, you're not aware of what is going on. You're not ...
   A. in the swim.
   B. on the agenda.
   C. in the picture.

5. He hasn't got the foggiest idea about the project.
   A. He's out of place.
   B. He is not in the swim.
   C. He's out at sea.

TASK 6: Business phrases to remember

Translate the words in brackets.

1. The first item on the (*Tagesordnung*) is whether we shall (*gewähren*) discount for (*Mengen*).
2. I think it's a bit early for a decision. I move for (*Vertagung*).
3. I suggest that we (*einrichten*) a subcommittee.
4. Let's have a (*Abstimmung*) on this (*Tagesordnungspunkt*).

Murphy's Laws

- Regardless of the length of the meeting, all important decisions will be made in the last five minutes before lunch or the end of the day.
- If a problem causes too many meetings, the meetings become more important than the problem.
- Meetings that you chair are infinitely better than those that you merely attend.
- The length of a meeting increases with the square of the number of people present.
- Whoever shouts loudest has the floor.
  Arthur Bloch

TASK 7: Magic squares – Around the house

Match the phrases (1, 2, 3) with the words in the box (A, B, C). Put the numbers in the magic squares. Columns and rows will all add up to the same number, **15**.

A. hat	D. kettle	G. floor
B. book	E. fence	H. nail
C. curtain	F. picture	I. chair

1. Our plans are now well advanced so I need to put you in the ★.
2. She held the ★ for over an hour and her audience was all ears.
3. You can't deceive him, he knows every trick in the ★.
4. His ideas are all terribly old ★.
5. You have got to make up your mind. You can't sit on the ★ forever.
6. Since I'm the oldest, I suppose it's my turn to take the ★.
7. You're bang on target. You've hit the ★ on the head.
8. It's four o'clock and a Friday. I think it's time to bring down the ★ on this meeting.
9. I'm pretty well familiar with British law. European law is a different ★ of fish.

A =	B =	C =
D =	E =	F =
G =	H =	I =

NEGOTIATING
VERHANDELN

Negotiating is a skill that can be learned, but often isn't. Two parties have two different positions and want to achieve at a result together. Ideally they should arrive at a win-win situation where both sides can profit from the agreement. More often than not one or the other party wants to get some sort of advantage. It can become bitter and then we have win-lose or lose-lose situations.

Bird's eye view

1. Strategy and tactics	*Strategie und Taktik*
2. At the negotiating table	*Am Verhandlungstisch*
3. Coming to an agreement	*Sich einigen*
4. Phrases for negotiators	*Ausdrücke für Unterhändler*

Time for a smile

An Irish businessman went to see his doctor about his sexual problems.
"You've been working too hard. Get some exercise," the doctor advised. "Try riding a bike a few miles every day."
Four days later, the doctor received a telephone call from the man. "How are you this morning? Has your sex life improved?" he asked.
"How would I know? I'm seventy miles from home," was the angry reply.

A — A FIRST TASTE OF idioms

1. Strategy and tactics – *Strategie und Taktik*

strike while the iron's hot	*das Eisen schmieden, solange es heiß ist*
change one's tack	*seinen Kurs ändern*
have several irons in the fire	*mehrere Eisen im Feuer haben*

Test your memory: What's the *woggle*?

1. If I don't get that job, it doesn't matter. I've several other *woggles* in the fire.
2. The sales strategy is not successful. It's time to *woggle* our tack.
3. Don't wait! Strike while the *woggle* is hot.

2. At the negotiating table – *Am Verhandlungstisch*

do an about-turn	*eine Kehrtwendung machen*
not see the wood for the trees	*den Wald vor lauter Bäumen nicht sehen*
be in a tight corner	*schwer in Bedrängnis sein*

Test your memory: Compare and correct the mistakes

1. There are hundreds of opportunities around. You *can't see the trees for the woods*.
2. We were losing money. Then we *did a turn-about*. Now, we're in the black.
3. There's not enough money to pay the trainers. We are *in a tight corner*.

Continued

turn up trumps	*überlegen sein*
meet one's match	*seinen Meister finden*
come to the crunch	*hart auf hart gehen*

Test your memory

1. The team *t_____* up *t_____* on the day. They were better than expected.
2. He thought he was the best driver, but he's *m_____* his *m_____* in Tom.
3. When it *c_____* to the *c_____* he easily loses control.

3. Coming to an agreement – *Sich einigen*

be within a whisker of an agreement	*eine Einigung ist zum Greifen nahe*
save the day	*die Situation retten*
take the consequences	*die Konsequenzen tragen*

Test your memory: The words in *italics* are in the wrong sentences

1. John will have to take the *whisker* if he continues to do shabby work.
2. Through a clever strategy we finally *saved* the consequences.
3. The two firms are now within a *day* of agreeing on a deal.

Time for a smile

To help a new salesman become familiar with the company's product the sales manager suggested he demonstrate it to his wife. The next morning the manager asked, "How did the presentation go?" "I did what you told me," said the salesman, "and when I finished, I asked my wife, 'Would you buy it?' She said, 'Yes'! When I asked her why, she replied, 'Because I love you'!"

B   The main COURSE

1. Strategy and tactics – *Strategie und Taktik*

put out / stretch out one's feelers	*seine Fühler ausstrecken; das Terrain sondieren*
see how the land lies	*die Lage peilen*
get the lay of the land	*die Lage einschätzen / peilen; einen Überblick bekommen*
try another tack	*es anders versuchen*
go it alone	*einen Alleingang machen*
have a free hand	*freie Hand haben*
give someone carte blanche / a free hand	*jemandem Blankovollmacht geben*
act as someone's straw man	*für jemanden als Strohmann agieren*
keep one's options open	*sich alle Optionen offen halten*
play / stall for time	*auf Zeit spielen; versuchen, Zeit zu gewinnen*
play it safe	*auf Nummer sicher gehen*
have more than one string to one's bow	*mehrere Eisen im Feuer haben*
play the wrong card	*auf die falsche Karte setzen*
A bird in the hand is worth two in the bush.	*Der Spatz in der Hand ist besser als die Taube auf dem Dach.*
Don't put all your eggs in one basket.	*Setze nicht alles auf eine Karte.*
Nothing ventured, nothing gained.	*Wer nicht wagt, der nicht gewinnt.*
You can't have the best of both worlds.	*Man kann nicht alles haben. Entweder – oder!*

Idioms overheard

At the conference table. Stephan (**S**) from Druva, Ron (**R**) from SUP:

S: So we*'ve put out a few feelers* and we think we can get this software cheaper.

R: Don't even think about it. You*'ll be playing the wrong card.*

S: Well, we want to play it safe. We shouldn't *put all our eggs in one basket.* Not even your basket.

R: Of course, I understand you want to *keep your options open,* but ...

2. At the negotiating table – *Am Verhandlungstisch*

The unprepared negotiator

sit on the fence	*sich abwartend / unschlüssig verhalten*
play a waiting game	*die Ereignisse abwarten; auf Zeit setzen*
drag one's feet	*etwas (absichtlich) hinauszögern*
sit back and do nothing	*die Hände in den Schoß legen*
lay / put one's cards on the table	*seine Karten auf den Tisch legen*
jump / leap at an offer	*sich auf ein Angebot stürzen*
gamble on someone's support	*auf jemandes Unterstützung setzen*
drop a hint	*eine Andeutung machen*
play both ends against the middle; play both sides	*ein Doppelspiel treiben*
play into someone's hands	*jemandem in die Hände spielen*
aim below the belt	*unter die Gürtellinie zielen*
blow hot and cold	*mal hü, mal hott sagen; sich mal so und mal so entscheiden*
overshoot the mark	*etwas zu weit treiben*
take a gamble	*ein Risiko eingehen*
split hairs	*Haarspalterei betreiben*
beat a retreat	*den Rückzug antreten*
meet one's match	*seinen Meister finden*
not be in the same league as someone	*sich mit jemandem nicht messen können*
not be able to touch someone	*jemandem nicht das Wasser reichen können*

have one's back to the wall	*mit dem Rücken zur Wand stehen*
bark up the wrong tree	*auf der falschen Fährte / dem Holzweg sein*
shoot oneself in the foot; shoot an own goal	*ein Eigentor schießen*
cut no ice with someone	*keinen Eindruck auf jemanden machen; jemanden kalt lassen*
double-cross someone	*ein Doppelspiel mit jemandem treiben*
bow out	*einen Rückzieher machen*
do a U-turn / flip-flop	*eine Kehrtwendung vollziehen*
draw a line under something	*einen Schlussstrich unter etwas ziehen*
throw in the towel / sponge	*das Handtuch werfen; sich geschlagen geben*
burn one's bridges / boats	*alle Brücken hinter sich abbrechen*
get into hot water	*sich in die Brennnesseln setzen*
get into deep water / a scrape	*aufs Glatteis geraten*
These arguments are cut and dried.	*Das sind Argumente von der Stange.*

Idioms overheard

Sales director Needy (**N**) and his chief salesman, Mr Shark (**S**):

N: I won't *beat about the bush*. It's going to be difficult at Lumy. They feel we*'re dragging our feet*.

S: I'm not so pessimistic. We *haven't burnt our bridges yet*.

N: No, but we*'ve got our backs to the wall*. Our after-sales at Lumy was lousy.

S: Okay, so it's time to *beat a retreat* and find a brand new strategy.

The well-prepared negotiator

keep the ball rolling	*im Gespräch bleiben*
be as cool as a cucumber	*einen kühlen Kopf bewahren*
mean business	*es ernst meinen*
keep one's cards close to one's chest	*sich nicht in die Karten schauen lassen*
play one's cards right	*seine Karten richtig ausspielen*
keep one's eyes peeled / skinned	*wie ein Schießhund aufpassen; die Augen offen halten*
guard one's patch	*an den eigenen Vorteil denken*
hold one's horses	*sich bremsen; sich beherrschen; sich zurückhalten*
know every trick in the trade	*mit allen Wassern gewaschen sein*
put oneself into someone's shoes	*sich in jemandes Lage versetzen*
play ball with someone	*mit jemandem mitspielen*
play games with someone	*mit jemandem sein Spiel treiben*
shoot questions at someone	*jemanden mit Fragen bombardieren*
get / have / gain the upper hand over someone	*Oberhand über jemanden gewinnen*
have someone in one's pocket	*jemanden in der Tasche haben*
pull the carpet from under someone's feet	*jemandem den Boden unter den Füßen wegziehen*
catch someone with their pants / trousers down	*jemanden eiskalt erwischen*
catch someone napping	*jemanden überrumpeln*
not touch an offer with a bargepole	*ein Angebot nicht mit der Kohlenzange anfassen*
drive a wedge between	*einen Keil treiben zwischen*
turn the tables on someone	*den Spieß umdrehen*
play for high stakes	*viel riskieren; um hohe Einsätze spielen*
pick the cherries from the cake	*die Rosinen aus dem Kuchen picken*
put the screws on someone	*jemanden unter Druck setzen*
put the squeeze on	*jemanden erpressen*

twist someone round one's little finger	*jemanden um den kleinen Finger wickeln*
hang on like grim death	*nicht locker lassen; verbissen festhalten an*
cost what it may	*koste es, was es wolle*
have someone over a barrel	*jemanden in der Zange haben*
It's easier to get blood out of a stone.	*Es ist einfacher, einen Stier zu melken.*
The boot is now on the other foot.	*Jetzt ist der Spieß umgedreht; die Sache sieht ganz anders aus.*
You could have heard a pin drop.	*Man hätte eine Stecknadel fallen hören können.*

Idioms overheard

Kurz (**K**) from Purchasing discusses the price with a supplier (**S**):

K: And as I said, if you *play ball with us*, we'll play ball with you.

S: Well, you really *caught me napping* with your new centralized purchasing system. I didn't expect it.

K: We had to *play our cards close to our chests*. Nobody had to know, but I hope you'll go along with us.

S: And I hope you understand we have *to guard our patch*, too

---

Food for thought

Education is when you read the fine print.
Experience is what you get if you don't.

3. Coming to an agreement – *Sich einigen*

do business with	*Geschäfte machen mit*
put someone at ease	*jemandes Nerven beruhigen*
pour oil on troubled waters	*die Wogen glätten; die Gemüter beschwichtigen*
show one's colours	*Farbe bekennen*
labour a point	*auf etwas herumreiten*
thrash out a question	*eine Frage bis ins Detail ausdiskutieren*
break the deadlock	*den toten Punkt überwinden*
break the ice	*das Eis brechen; einen Durchbruch erzielen*
listen to reason	*Vernunft annehmen*
settle one's differences	*seine Meinungsverschiedenheiten beilegen*
count the cost of	*die Folgen bedenken*
clear the way	*den Weg frei machen*
meet someone halfway	*jemandem auf halbem Wege entgegenkommen*
strike / reach a compromise	*einen Kompromiss schließen*
come to terms with someone	*handelseinig werden*
strike a bargain	*ein gutes Geschäft machen*
make a deal with	*ein Geschäft abschließen mit*
read between the lines	*zwischen den Zeilen lesen*
sign on the dotted line	*etwas unterzeichnen*
carry out a contract to the letter	*einen Vertrag buchstabengetreu erfüllen*
It's in the bag.	*Das Geschäft ist unter Dach und Fach.*
There are (no) strings attached.	*Es ist kein Haken an der Sache.*

4. Phrases for negotiators – *Ausdrücke für Unterhändler*

not hold water	*nicht stichhaltig sein*
negotiate till the cows come home	*bis zum Sankt-Nimmerleins-Tag / Jüngsten Gericht verhandeln*
stand to reason	*einleuchten; logisch / selbstverständlich sein*
stick to the point	*beim Thema bleiben*
that's beyond the pale	*das ist indiskutabel / nicht akzeptabel*
be as different as chalk and cheese	*grundverschieden / himmelweit auseinander sein*
be a different kettle of fish	*eine ganz andere Sache sein*
clinch / strike / wrap up / sew up / stitch up a deal	*ein Geschäft / einen Vertrag unter Dach und Fach bringen*
read someone's thoughts	*jemandes Gedanken lesen*
get down to brass tacks.	*Nägel mit Köpfen machen; zur Hauptsache kommen.*
I don't buy that!	*Das kaufe ich Ihnen nicht ab!*
It's your best bet.	*Das ist Beste, was Sie tun können.*
There's a catch to it.	*Die Sache hat einen Haken.*
Let's have less talk and more action.	*Der Worte sind genug gewechselt.*
You scratch my back and I'll scratch yours.	*Eine Hand wäscht die andere.*
That is not to be sneezed at.	*Das ist nicht zu verachten.*
a going concern	*ein gut gehendes Geschäft*
a gold mine	*eine Goldgrube*
His honesty sticks out a mile.	*Die Ehrlichkeit steht ihm ins Gesicht geschrieben.*
The ball is in your court.	*Jetzt sind Sie am Zug.*
It's all said and done.	*Es ist alles gesagt worden.*
That's right up my alley street.	*Das ist genau mein Fall. Das ist was für mich.*
Give him an inch and he'll take a mile.	*Reiche ihm den kleinen Finger und er nimmt die ganze Hand.*
You can't have your cake and eat it!	*Du kannst nur eines von beiden haben! Entweder – oder!*
There are no two ways about it.	*Da gibt's gar keinen Zweifel.*

Idioms overheard

In the Purchasing Department. Stephan (**S**) is discussing strategy with Kurt (**K**):

S: Well, this supplier is important to us, but we're *in deadlock*.

K: Look, *at the end of the day* we have to find a compromise. We need Tychotruns.

S: Well, *the ball's in their court*. We've offered them three quarters of our business.

K: Get them to *sign on the dotted line*. That's all we need.

Time for a smile

The greatest salesman in the world was the guy who brought a girl up to his apartment to see his stamp collection – and he sold her 20 stamps.

C Idioms AT WORK

TASK 1: Idioms in poem

Find the word that rhymes.

I tried to clear the way
For an agreement – cost what it _____.
They gambled on the enterprise
Refused to strike a _____.
And finally I had to beat
A disappointed slow _____.

TASK 2: You keep it in your fridge

Put them where they belong.

cake	cherries	cucumber
cheese	eggs	fish

1. He never loses his temper, he's always as cool as a _____.
2. I don't put all my _____ into one basket. I usually have more strings to my bow.
3. He wants a regular income but doesn't want to work. He can't have his _____ and eat it!
4. We've offered you a package tour. It's take it or leave it. You can't just pick the _____ from the cake.
5. I'm afraid this is not what we previously agreed on. This proposal's a very different kettle of _____.
6. The quality you're offering us now is as different as chalk and _____ from the one you sent us a week ago.

TASK 3: Idioms from the animal world

bird	cat	donkey
cows	feelers	horse

1. I'll try to put out some _____ to test people's reactions to the idea.
2. This product is not exactly what I'd call a money spinner. I'm afraid we bet on the wrong _____.
3. Let's stop betting now rather than risk losing everything. A _____ in the hand is worth two in the bush.
4. You can talk till the _____ come home, you'll never make me change my mind.
5. Don't do anything rash. Let's wait and see which way the _____ jumps.
6. What a bore. He could talk the hind legs off a _____.

TASK 4: Rhyme Verbs

The verbs in the idioms are rhyme verbs. Do you remember?

1. Don't _ _ ay a waiting game. _ ay your cards on the table.
2. Don't _ i_ on the fence and _ _ _ i _ hairs.
3. When you _ ee _ your match, you'd better _ ea _ a retreat.
4. He _ u_ _ e _ his bridges and _ u_ _ e _ up trumps.
5. Don't _ _ o _ hot and cold – _ _ o _ your colours.

TASK 5: The good negotiator and clothes

The first letters have been done for you.

1. A good negotiator never aims below the b_____.
2. He is able to put himself in his partner's_____.
3. You'll never catch him with his t_____ down.
4. It's very difficult to have him in your p_____.

Time for a smile

Sir Harry Lauder, one of Scotland's most famous sons, was once interviewed by a reporter who asked him how he had managed to amass such a large fortune.

"Well, it's a long story," he replied, "and since we have no need of light while I'm telling it, let me blow out the candle."

"I don't think you need to tell me any more," replied the reporter.

TASK 6: Magic squares – They grow on your body

Match the phrases (1, 2, 3) with the words in the box (A, B, C). Put the numbers in the magic squares. Columns and rows will all add up to the same number, **15**.

A. whisker	D. foot	G. hairs
B. back	E. hands	H. feet
C. chest	F. eyes	I. finger

1. When he became boss himself he found that the boot was on the other ★.
2. I wish I could read his thoughts, but he keeps his cards close to his ★.
3. If we buy up their shares we might cut the ground from under their ★.
4. He is a lousy negotiator and easy to twist round one's little ★.
5. By selling our shares we'll play into our competitor's ★.
6. The two firms are now within a ★ of agreeing on a deal.
7. Because they refused to grant him a loan he had his ★ to the wall.
8. Stop splitting ★. There are almost no differences between the two offers.
9. Be very careful. New euro bills might be forged, so keep your ★ peeled for any counterfeit money.

A =	B =	C =
D =	E =	F =
G =	H =	I =

A COMPETITIVE WORLD
EINE WELT IM WETTSTREIT

A few years ago companies and decision-makers were concerned with quality in all its facets. Nowadays, cost and competition seem to be the buzzwords. More energy is spent worrying about what our competitors are doing than getting on with our jobs. Read on for idioms on the subject.

Bird's eye view

1. Struggling with competitors	*Mit Konkurrenten kämpfen*
2. Getting the edge over the competition	*Oberhand über die Konkurrenz gewinnen*
3. Winning and losing	*Gewinnen und verlieren*

Time for a smile

A woman lion tamer had the cats under such control that they took a lump of sugar from her lips on command. When a sceptic yelled "Anyone can do that!" the ringmaster came over and asked him, "Would you like to try it?"

"Certainly," said the man. "But first get those crazy lions out of there."

A — A FIRST TASTE of idioms

1. Struggling with competitors – Mit Konkurrenten kämpfen

be in the rat-race	*im wirtschaftlichen Überlebenskampf stehen*
be neck and neck	*Kopf an Kopf liegen*
set the fashion	*den Ton angeben*

Test your memory: Correct the spelling mistakes

1. Nickers Sports are certainly *getting the fashion* in sports footwear.
2. Working seventy hours a week, trying to keep up with competitors. I'm tired of *being in the cat-race*.
3. Lentingua and Combinations *are neck at neck* in their attempt to get Heidelberg Concrete as a client.

2. Getting the edge over the competition – Oberhand über die Konkurrenz gewinnen

mop up a firm	*eine Firma schlucken*
hold all the aces	*alle Trümpfe in der Hand halten*
catch someone on the hop	*jemanden auf dem falschen Fuß erwischen*

Test your memory: Careful! Words have been exchanged!

1. SUP have their software in all the companies. As a monopolist they *catch* all the aces.
2. Heidelberg Printing Presses *are hopping up* all the competition. Nobody can touch them.
3. The rush for fuel *hold* petrol companies *on the mop*.

3. Winning and losing – *Gewinnen und verlieren*

have the edge on / over someone	*einen Vorteil gegenüber jemandem haben, jemandem voraus / über sein*
be second to none	*unvergleichlich / unübertroffen sein*
run rings around	*jemanden mühelos schlagen*

Test your memory: What's the *woggle?*

1. The recent performance of our company *is second to woggle.*
2. We were able to *run woggles around* our toughest competitor.
3. Microsoft definitely *had the woggle on* Apple.

B The main COURSE

1. Struggling with competitors – *Mit Konkurrenten kämpfen*

mount an advertising campaign	*einen Werbefeldzug starten*
get a head start	*einen guten Start hinlegen*
breathe down someone's neck	*jemandem dicht auf den Fersen sein*
hold one's own against	*sich behaupten gegen*
a neck-and-neck race	*ein Kopf-an-Kopf-Rennen*
gain ground	*an Boden gutmachen*
draw level with	*mit jemandem gleichziehen*
gain a foothold in the market	*auf dem Markt Fuß fassen*
drive someone into a corner	*jemanden in die Ecke treiben*
be a rough customer	*ein übler Kunde sein*
come to grips with something	*etwas in den Griff kriegen*
go to any lengths	*vor nichts zurückschrecken; nichts unversucht lassen*
act out of hand	*sich nicht an die Spielregeln halten*

Idioms overheard

René (**R**) talking to Michael (**M**), his lawyer:

R: Our major customer is *acting out of hand*. Sometimes they pay on time, sometimes they don't.

M: But through all this business with them you've *gained a foothold in the market*, and without needing to advertise.

R: I hear what you're saying, but I'd *go to any lengths* to safeguard the future of our company.

2. Getting the edge over the competitor – *Oberhand über die Konkurrenz gewinnen*

meet a challenge	*sich einer Herausforderung / Aufgabe stellen*
keep one jump ahead of the competition.	*der Konkurrenz einen Schritt voraus sein*
catch off guard / unawares	*jemanden unvorbereitet / kalt erwischen*
catch on the hop	*auf dem falschen Fuß erwischen*
get / have an edge over someone	*einen Vorteil gegenüber jemandem haben; im Vorteil sein*
get the better of someone	*jemandem den Rang ablaufen; die Oberhand gewinnen*
get the upper hand	*die Oberhand gewinnen*
wipe the floor with a competitor	*mit einem Konkurrenten den Boden aufwischen / Schlitten fahren*
be ahead of the game	*einen Schritt voraus sein*
have / get one's foot in the door	*einen Fuß in der Tür haben / in die Tür bekommen*
be one up on someone	*jemandem einen Schritt voraus sein*
have a good thing going	*gut im Rennen liegen; eine gute Sache laufen haben*
turn the heat on	*unter Druck setzen; den Druck verstärken*

Idioms overheard

René (**R**) discusses competitors with Bob (**B**), his shareholder:

B: Well, Unilingua have really *caught you on the hop*.

R: I know. They've moved in on our major customer. But we've *got a head start on* them.

B: Nonetheless, they've got *a foot in the door* and I'm worried about my investment.

3. Winning and losing – *Gewinnen und verlieren*

trade on the gullibility of the public	*auf die Gutgläubigkeit der Öffentlichkeit spekulieren*
leave someone out in the cold	*jemanden im Regen stehen lassen*
come out ahead / on top of someone	*vor jemandem durchs Ziel gehen / besser sein*
come off second-best	*den Kürzeren ziehen*
go one better	*eine Nummer besser sein*
defend oneself tooth and nail	*sich mit Zähnen und Klauen verteidigen*
turn the tables	*den Spieß umdrehen; das Glück wenden*
develop in a free-for-all	*in wildes Gerangel ausarten*
run a competitor into the ground	*einen Konkurrenten vernichten*
beat someone hollow	*jemanden vernichtend schlagen*
take by storm	*im Sturme erobern*
wipe something off the map	*etwas ausradieren / dem Erdboden gleichmachen*
give it one's best shot	*sein Bestes versuchen / geben*
have time out	*eine Auszeit nehmen; eine Pause machen*
come to blows	*handgreiflich werden*
go at each other hammer and tongs	*(sich) streiten, dass die Fetzen fliegen*
bring up the rear	*das Schlusslicht bilden*

mess someone up (sl)	*jemanden fertig machen*
give someone a licking	*jemanden verprügeln; jemandem*
	eine Niederlage verpassen
not come within a mile of the competitor	*nicht den Hauch einer Chance gegen die Konkurrenz haben*
jockey for position	*sich um eine gute Position rangeln*
be on the bench	*auf der Reservebank sitzen*
be in the running	*im Rennen sein*
be out of the running	*nicht mehr im Rennen sein*
tilt at windmills	*gegen Windmühlen kämpfen*
throw in / up the sponge	*das Handtuch werfen*
throw in the towel	*das Handtuch werfen*
The game is up.	*Das Spiel ist aus.*

Idioms overheard

Private conversation between Personnel Manager (**P**) and Bossybitch(**B**) of Language Consultants GmbH:

P: So your Language Consultants GmbH were *left out in the cold* because your prices were too high.

B: But what about quality? Unilingua *don't come within a mile of us* concerning results.

P: You're out of date. Since Lopez and his purchasing philosophy it's all about price. Wake up or you'll *miss the boat*.

Time for a smile

A salesman was staying overnight in a country town. Out of sheer boredom he opened the bible that was provided in all motel rooms. Inside he found a business card with a message: "If you are bored and lonely, if you desire some warm and comfort, ring Susie, 58-5573."

C   Idioms AT WORK

TASK 1:   Do you remember the idiom?

1. The market place for new anti-aging drugs is nothing more than a ✎.
   A. free-to-everybody   **B.** free-to-all   **C.** free-for-all

2. The publication of the test results of the drug Viagry caught the pharmaceutical company ABS ✎.
   A. as a sop   **B.** on the top   **C.** on the hop

3. The ABS went to great ✎ to keep the test results secret.
   A. lengths   **B.** levels   **C.** levers

4. Some managers, who had a bad conscience about the by-effects of Viagry, gained the ✎.
   A. lower arm   **B.** upper leg   **C.** upper hand

5. Finally, the Board threw ✎ and withdrew the drug from the market.
   A. up the handkerchief   **B.** in the towel   **C.** down the sponge

TASK 2:   Which idiom goes with which definition?

1. come / get to grips with something
2. turn the tables on someone
3. jockey for a position
4. wipe the floor with someone
5. keep one jump ahead of someone
6. hold one's own against

A. maintain one's position against competition and not become weaker
B. remain one stage ahead of a rival
C. defeat someone thoroughly in an argument or a contest
D. try by every available means to gain an advantage or a favour
E. reverse a situation so as to put oneself in a position of superiority
F. begin to deal seriously with a problem, challenge, etc

TASK 3: Say it in English

1. Last year we (*starteten einen Werbefeldzug*) for our new electric scooter for kids.
2. It was the first scooter of its kind and so we (*gewannen einen Vorsprung vor*) our competitors.
3. However, FwS (Fun with Sun) developed a scooter driven by solar energy and (*fasste Fuß auf*) on the market.
4. At first we were able (*uns zu behaupten gegen*) FwS.
5. But soon we felt (*dass sie uns dicht auf den Fersen waren*).
6. It was an extremely hot and sunny year so FwS (*war uns gegenüber im Vorteil*).
7. In order not to (*aus dem Rennen zu sein*) we're developing a skate board propelled by solar energy.
8. And if we manage to integrate the solar cells in a T-shirt we'll (*FwS vernichtend schlagen*), I bet my bottom dollar on it.

TASK 4: Tim, the 'Yes-man'

1

Tom: Well, I think that with our solar T-shirt we'll *be one up on* FwS (Fun with Sun).

Tim: Of course, we'll *be one* _____ *ahead of* them.

2

Tom: And in a year, FwS won't *be in the running* anymore.

Tim: Of course, they'll be _____ _____ *the running*.

3

Tom: And our solar skate board will *run FwS into the ground*.

Tim: Yes, we'll *beat them* _____, that's for sure.

4

Tom: FwS will disappear from the market.

Tim: Yes, we'll _____ *them off the* _____ .

TASK 5: Magic squares – Sporting idioms

Match the phrases (1, 2, 3) with the words (A, B, C). Put the numbers in the magic squares. Columns and rows will all add up to the same number, **15**.

A. bench	D. towel	G. sponge
B. level	E. game	H. mile
C. running	F. shot	I. jockey

1. FwS's (Fun with Sun) solar scooter doesn't come within a ★ of our new SS (Solar Skateboard).
2. By the way, their best skater is injured and will be sitting on the ★.
3. Bob the Magnificent gave it his best ★, but it simply wasn't good enough for Ron the Hulk.
4. Their ★ is up, they used a scooter that had been souped up.
5. FwS is no longer in the ★.
6. They threw up the ★ before they had to undergo a doping test.
7. If they hadn't thrown in the ★ they would have been disqualified.
8. FwS have to ★ for position on the market with SS.
9. FwS won't draw ★ with SS however hard they might try.

A =	B =	C =
D =	E =	F =
G =	H =	I =

LAW AND ORDER
RECHT UND GESETZ

The rules of society and the breaking of them seems to preoccupy us perhaps more than anything. Crime is big nowadays, punishment is confusing, at least for the majority of us. People who break the law don't know what to expect. Kill someone, you only get a few years; steal some money, offend the state you can be put away for decades. It's all a bit upside down, isn't it?

Bird's eye view

1. Legalese and lawyers	*Juristenjargon und Juristen*
2. Law-abiding citizens	*Gesetzestreue Bürger*
3. Minor offences	*Kleinere Gesetzesübertretungen*
4. Burglars, muggers and murderers	*Einbrecher, Schläger und Mörder*
5. Justice, trial, punishment	*Gerechtigkeit, Prozess, Strafe*
6. Getting away with it	*Ungestraft davonkommen*

Time for a smile

After the judge had found a Friesian guilty of robbery, he asked the criminal if he could pay the costs of the trial. "I'm afraid not," said the accused, "I've given all my money to my lawyer and three of the jury."

A A FIRST TASTE of idioms

1. Legalese and lawyers – *Juristenjargon und Juristen*

do it by the book	*sich genau an die Vorschriften halten*
find a loophole in the law	*eine Lücke im Gesetz finden*
send someone up the river [US]	*jemanden verkaufen, in den Knast schicken*

Test your memory: Find the mistake – it's a rhyme word

1. My friend Michael, the lawyer, explained to me that he made a lot of money by *finding coopholes in the paw*.
2. Mick swindles his taxes. When they catch up with him they'll *rend him up the liver*.
3. We are proud to announce that we *did* everything *by the cook* at Combe-nations GmbH.

2. Law-abiding citizens – *Gesetzestreue Bürger*

stay on the straight and narrow	*auf dem Pfad der Tugend bleiben*
(never) put a foot wrong	*(nie) etwas Falsches tun / sagen*
be as clean as a whistle	*eine weiße Weste haben*

Test your memory: Can you read it without the vowels?

1. In all his years as a teacher Jim never *pxt* a *fxxt wrxng* until Sally came along.
2. After he left prison David promised his mother he would *stxx* on the *strxxght* and *nxrrxw*.
3. The police raided Tom's flat searching for hash, but Tom was as *clxxn* as a *whxstlx*.

3. Minor offences – *Kleinere Gesetzesübertretungen*

grease someone's palm	*jemanden schmieren / bestechen*
stink to high heaven	*zum Himmel stinken*
fall off the back of a lorry	*Hehlerware sein*

Test your memory: What's the *woggle*?

1. The radios are certainly that cheap because they *fell off some woggle* somewhere.
2. I don't understand how you landed that contract. Did you *woggle* someone's *woggle* ?
3. I don't trust him. His excuses stink to *woggle* heaven .

4. Burglars, muggers and murderers – *Einbrecher, Schläger und Mörder*

have sticky fingers	*stehlen; lange Finger machen*
put the finger on someone	*jemanden erpressen*
bump someone off	*jemanden um die Ecke bringen*

Test your memory

1. He's been putting his _____ on Tim since he got that information about the drunk-driving conviction.
2. Be careful to keep the till locked. Ruth is said to have sticky _____.
3. In the thirties the mafia _____ everybody off who got in their way.

Time for a smile

McTavish was accused of having embezzled a large sum of money.
"Not guilty," said the judge after a lengthy trial.
"Does that mean I can keep the money?" asked McTavish.

5. Justice, trial, punishment – *Gerechtigkeit, Prozess, Strafe*

get sent down	*mit Gefängnis – Gerechtigkeit, Prozess, Strafe bestraft werden*
be in the clink (sl)	*im Kittchen sitzen*
run someone in	*jemanden einlochen*

Test your memory: Use the above idioms

1. David? Hmm, I don't know exactly. I think he's been *in prison* for more than ten years.
2. What did he *go to prison* for? – Grievous bodily harm. My God!
3. The police *arrested him* after a car-chase and a series of interviews with the local radio.

6. Getting away with it – *Ungestraft davonkommen*

get off scot-free	*ungestraft davonkommen*
cut and run (sl)	*abhauen; Reißaus nehmen; auf und davon rennen*
bluff one's way out	*sich herausreden; durchmogeln*

Test your memory

1. Actually, Jim stole that money, but through lack of proof he's got off _____ .
2. The students reported what he's been saying. I don't think he can _____ his way out of that.
3. When he saw the balance sheet of the company, he simply _____ and run and left me with the debts.

B   The main COURSE

1. Legalese and lawyers – *Juristenjargon und Juristen*

go by the book	*sich an die Vorschriften / das Gesetz halten*
do something in the name of the law	*etwas im Namen des Gesetzes tun*
be the arm of the law	*der Arm des Gesetzes sein*
come into force	*in Kraft treten; rechtskräftig werden*
sign something away	*etwas überschreiben*
have something in black and white	*etwas schwarz auf weiß haben*
go to law with someone	*jemanden verklagen; gegen jemanden prozessieren*
have someone up	*jemanden vor den Kadi schleppen*
take someone to court	*jemanden vor Gericht bringen*
get caught up in the machinery / labyrinth of the law	*in die Mühlen der Justiz geraten*
get caught up in the bureaucratic machine	*in die Mühlen der Bürokratie geraten*
the law of the jungle	*das Gesetz des Dschungels*
be an open and shut case	*ein klarer Fall sein*
bend the law	*das Gesetz beugen; die Vorschriften umgehen*
evade the law	*ein Gesetz umgehen; sich den Bestimmungen entziehen*
cop a plea	*sich schuldig bekennen, um das Strafmaß gering zu halten*
face the music	*die Suppe auslöffeln*
extenuating circumstances	*mildernde Umstände*
be out on bail	*auf Kaution frei sein*
throw the book at someone	*jemanden zur Höchststrafe verurteilen*

Idioms overheard

Bob (**B**) and Ron (**R**) discuss legal problems:

B: It's here *in black and white*. The new laws on pseudo-self-employment have come into effect.

R: Well, I feel it's more *the law of the jungle* that's in effect here in Germany. How can I check if my suppliers have more than one customer.

B: I don't know, but I do know if you get it wrong they'll *throw the book at* you.

2. Law-abiding citizens – *Gesetzestreue Bürger*

have a clean slate / record	*eine reine Weste haben*
keep one's nose clean	*sauber bleiben*
be safe from suspicion	*über jeden Verdacht erhaben sein*
be as clean as a whistle	*eine weiße Weste haben*
be as straight as a die	*anständig und gesetzestreu sein*
(never) put a foot wrong	*sich nie etwas zuschulden kommen lassen, nie etwas falsch machen*
get to the bottom of something	*einer Sache auf den Grund gehen*
be a true blue	*ein echter und aufrichtiger Engländer sein*
bring / come to light	*ans Licht / an die Öffentlichkeit bringen / gelangen*
stick to the letter of the law	*am Buchstaben des Gesetzes kleben*
keep out of trouble	*sich nichts zuschulden kommen lassen*

3. Minor offences – *Kleinere Gesetzesübertretungen*

do a breath test	*in das Röhrchen blasen*
drunk in charge of a vehicle; drunken driving	*Trunkenheit am Steuer*
go through a red light	*ein Rotlicht überfahren*
get into trouble with the police	*es mit der Polizei zu tun kriegen*

knock something off (sl)	*etwas klauen*
have sticky fingers	*gerne lange Finger machen*
swipe / nick / pinch something (sl)	*etwas klauen / klemmen / stibitzen*
escape by the skin of one's teeth	*etwas mit knapper Not schaffen*
commit shoplifting	*Ladendiebstahl begehen*
have one's hand in the till	*die Finger in der Ladenkasse haben*
be in the soup	*in der Tinte / in der Patsche sitzen; im Schlamassel stecken*
pull the wool over someone's eyes	*jemanden hinters Licht führen*
pull a job	*ein Ding drehen*
pin the blame on someone	*jemandem etwas in die Schuhe schieben*
blow the lid off a scandal	*einen Skandal aufdecken*
evade taxes	*Steuern hinterziehen*
moonlight	*schwarzarbeiten*
stink to high heaven	*zum Himmel stinken*
dirty one's hands	*sich die Hände schmutzig machen*
line one's pockets	*sich bereichern; in die eigene Tasche wirtschaften*
be a loan shark	*ein Kredithai sein*
grease someone's palm	*jemanden bestechen / schmieren*
do the dirty on someone	*jemanden linken / reinlegen*
catch someone red-handed	*jemanden auf frischer Tat / in flagranti ertappen*
catch someone in the act	*auf frischer Tat ertappen*
come out in the wash	*im Laufe der Zeit ans Tageslicht gelangen*
have a skeleton in the closet	*eine Leiche im Keller haben*
What a bunch of crooks!	*Diese Gauner!*
Let sleeping dogs lie.	*Schlafende Hunde soll man nicht wecken.*
A leopard can't change his spots.	*Die Katze lässt das Mausen nicht.*

Idioms overheard

The problem with our society nowadays is that nobody's really honest. We get our good example starting at the top. Our politicians try to *pull the wool over our eyes* wherever they can. They play games with us and stupid as we are, we hardly notice it. It's far too rare that political scandals actually *come out in the wash*. And more often than not our leaders are *lining their own pockets* in one way or another.

4. Burglars, muggers and murderers – *Einbrecher, Schläger und Mörder*

give someone a good hiding	*jemandem die Hucke voll hauen*
put someone's face out of joint (sl)	*jemandem die Fresse polieren*
beat someone up; clobber someone	*jemanden aufmischen / verprügeln*
keep a lookout	*Schmiere stehen*
rake something off	*etwas einsacken / abschöpfen*
beat someone black and blue	*jemanden grün und blau / windelweich schlagen*
rip someone off	*jemanden abzocken*
shake someone down	*jemanden erpressen*
stick someone up	*jemanden überfallen*
point a gun at someone's head	*das Messer an die Kehle setzen*
do someone in (sl)	*jemanden um die Ecke bringen*
blow someone away (sl)	*jemanden um die Ecke bringen*
make away / off with something	*sich etwas unter den Nagel reißen*

Time for a smile

I went to see a lawyer and said, "I need a lawyer to represent me competently and fairly." He said, "Make up your mind."

Idioms overheard

Did you hear that Peter got *beaten black and blue* when he was working late in his office the other evening. There were two of them. They really *put his face out of joint*. And after that they *made off with* all the money in the petty cash and in the safe. My goodness, nowadays it isn't even safe to sit and do your normal day's work.

5. Justice, trial, punishment – *Gerechtigkeit, Prozess, Strafe*

turn a blind eye to	*ein Auge zudrücken*
look the other way	*wegsehen; nicht hinsehen; bewusst nicht sehen wollen*
come clean about	*ein volles Geständnis ablegen*
be on the bench	*Richter sein*
take the stand / witness chair	*in den Zeugenstand treten; als Zeuge aussagen*
read someone his rights	*jemandem seine Rechte vorlesen*
suspect foul play	*ein Verbrechen vermuten*
cross-examine someone	*jemanden ins Kreuzverhör nehmen*
charge someone with breaking and entering	*jemanden des Einbruchdiebstahls beschuldigen*
pin a murder on someone	*jemandem einen Mord anhängen*
take the law into one's own hands	*das Gesetz in die eigenen Hände nehmen*
get a dose of one's own medicine	*etwas am eigenen Leib verspüren*
get one's come-uppance / get one's just dessert	*sein Fett / seine wohlverdiente Strafe bekommen*
run someone in	*jemanden einlochen*
go down for something	*für etwas mit Gefängnis bestraft werden*
be in the jug (sl)	*im Kittchen sitzen*
be in the slammer (sl)	*im Knast sein*
be inside	*im Kittchen sein*
sow mailbags	*Tüten kleben*
an eye for an eye, a tooth for a tooth	*Auge um Auge, Zahn um Zahn*

Idioms overheard

Ron (**R**) talks to Clifford (**C**), a childhood friend:

R: I'm sorry but in the end you *took the law into your own hands*.

C: And you're right. I was *charged with murder* and I did it. I *went down for* twenty-five years.

R: I think there were extenuating circumstances. It was a terrible thing your wife did.

C: It was *an eye for an eye and a tooth for a tooth*. But I regret it.

6. Getting away with it – *Ungestraft davonkommen*

get someone off the hook	*jemanden loseisen / freibekommen*
give someone the benefit of the doubt	*im Zweifelsfall für den Angeklagten sein*
get off lightly	*mit einem blauen Auge davonkommen*
get off scot-free	*ungestraft davonkommen*
get away with blue murder	*sich alles / jeden Unfug erlauben können*
give someone the slip	*jemandem entwischen*
have a close shave	*mit knapper Not entkommen*
get out of a jam / mess	*aus dem Schlamassel rauskommen*
jump bail	*die Kaution sausen lassen und verschwinden*
bluff one's way out	*sich herausreden / durchmogeln*
act as if nothing had happened	*so tun, als wäre nichts geschehen*
run for one's life	*um sein Leben rennen*
show them all a clean pair of heels	*sich davonmachen; seine Beine in die Hand nehmen*

 Idioms overheard

The police officer (**P**) speaking to Tom (**T**):

P: You *got off very lightly*. That was a case of tax evasion.

T: I know and I'm very grateful for the judge's decision.

P: You've *had a close shave* and be sure we'll be watching you. We believe you've *given us all the slip*, somehow. But we'll get you.

C   Idioms AT WORK

TASK 1:   Colourful idioms

Is it black, red, blue *or* white?

1. You'll lose you driver's license if you go through a _____ light again.
2. Politicians seem to get away with _____ murder in this country.
3. We'll have to wait until we get the judgement in _____ and _____.
4. The muggers beat the young tourist _____ and _____ .
5. Don't let the police catch you _____-handed.

TASK 2:   Tim, the 'Yes-man'

1.

Tom: Someone had his hand in the till. £40 are missing again. And it'll be me who has to report to the boss and *carry the can*.

Tim: Yes, it's unfair that it's always you who has to *face the* _____.

2.

Tom: I'll put up a video camera. Next time we'll *catch* the thief *in the act*.

Tim: That's it. We must catch him _____.

3.

Tom: And we'll *have him up for* repeated burglary and theft.

Tim: Of course, we'll _____ *him to court* immediately.

TASK 3:   Odd man out

Bob and Anne are discussing friend Ron.
Which phrase does not suit the context?

1. Did you hear? Ron has been caught in the act of shoplifting. –
   What was he trying to
   A. bump off?
   B. pinch?
   C. knock off?

2. An expensive watch, I think. – Well, that's Ron all over. I knew this would happen one day. I've told him again and again to
   A. keep out of trouble.
   B. keep his nose clean.
   C. keep a stiff upper lip.

3. And has Ron confessed to the shoplifting? – Of course not. He claims
   A. that he has a clean slate.
   B. that he's come clean about it.
   C. that he's as clean as a whistle.

4. Well, Bob, I think it would serve him right if
   A. he had to sow mailbags for a while.
   B. he got sent down for a couple of weeks.
   C. he got a dose of his own medicine.

5. I'm not so sure, Anne, with a good lawyer he will
   A. get his come-uppance.
   B. get off lightly.
   C. get off scot-free.

TASK 4: Verbs that go with law

We've helped with the first letter of the verb.

1. The director of the department store was determined to g _____ to law against Ron.
2. Ron fled to Brazil trying to e _____ the law, but he didn't escape the police.
3. He tried to bribe the Brazilian judge and was surprised to find out that Brazilian judges s _____ to the letter of the law.
4. However hard Ron's lawyer tried to b _____ and stretch the law, the German prosecutor didn't give in.

TASK 5: Magic squares – Body idioms

Match the phrases (1, 2, 3) with the parts of the body (A, B, C). Put the numbers in the magic squares. Columns and rows will all add up to the same number, **15**.

A. arm	D. face	G. palm
B. heels	E. fingers	H. nose
C. eye	F. foot	I. skin

1. If you keep your ★ clean, you'll do well in this firm.
2. He hoped to escape the long ★ of the law.
3. In all his years in the job I've never known him put a ★ wrong.
4. Judges often turn a blind ★ to minor breaches of law.
5. Ron's been told never to set foot into the department store again. They suspect him of having sticky ★.
6. He tried to grease the detective's ★. In vain!
7. The muggers threatened me put my ★ out of joint if I didn't give them 50 dollars.
8. Ron escaped the house detective by the ★ of his teeth.
9. The detective tried to catch up with him, but Ron showed him a clean pair of ★.

A =	B =	C =
D =	E =	F =
G =	H =	I =

Time for a smile

A defendant[1] in a lawsuit[2] involving a large sum of money was talking to his lawyer.

"If I lose the case, I'll be ruined. Would it help if I sent the judge a box of cigars?"

"Oh, no," said the lawyer. "This judge is a stickler[3] for ethical behaviour. A stunt like that would prejudice[4] him against you. In fact, you shouldn't even smile at the judge."

In the course of time, the judge rendered a decision in favour of the defendant.

As the defendant left the courthouse with his lawyer he said,

"Thanks for the tip about the cigars. It worked."

"I don't understand," said the lawyer.

"It's easy. I sent the cigars to the judge, but enclosed my opponent's business card."

Phrases to remember:
1 the defendant: *der Angeklagte*
2 lawsuit: *Gerichtsverfahren*
3 stickler: *Pedant*
4 prejudice against: *voreingenommen sein lassen gegen*

SMALL TALK
ZWANGLOSE GESPRÄCHE

It is important to understand the value and the place of small talk in communication with others. It is more than talking about the weather. It is a strategy carried out in a light and friendly way for exchanging unofficial but vital information for building personal relationships that may be important later.

Bird's eye view

1. Polite noises	*Höflichkeiten*
2. What to small-talk about	*Über was man so redet*
3. At the party	*Auf der Party*

Time for a smile

A journalist asked Sir Winston Churchill why he thought he had lived so long.
"Well, I'm convinced that it's the whisky and the cigars."
"Nothing else?" the journalist wanted to know.
"Just one more thing – cancelling my voyage on the Titanic."

A   A FIRST TASTE of idioms

1. Polite noises – *Höflichkeiten*

He's a chip off the old block.	*Der Apfel fällt nicht weit vom Stamm.*
have green fingers	*einen grünen Daumen haben*
pay someone a backhanded compliment	*jemandem ein zweideutiges Kompliment machen[1]*

Test your memory: Use the right idiom

1. Telling her she was the best in the class was an *ambiguous / ironic compliment* since they were all pretty bad.
2. Sue can grow absolutely anything. She's *a good gardener* alright.
3. She's *got her father's character*. Even that same twisted smile.

2. What to small-talk about – *Über was man so redet*

Everybody's health – *Das werte Befinden*

look like death warmed up	*wie eine Leiche auf Urlaub aussehen*
be on one's last legs	*auf dem letzten Loch pfeifen*
be as deaf as a post	*stocktaub sein*

Test your memory: What's the *woggle?*

1. My God, Bob, what's happened? You look like *woggle* warmed up.
2. This company's on its last *woggles*. We'd better start looking around.
3. If there's a fire alarm he won't hear it. He's as *woggle* as a post.

---

1 Example: "He's got more brains in his head than I've got in my little finger."

Gossip – *Klatsch*

Where've you been hiding?	*Wo hast du die ganze Zeit gesteckt?*
have a shotgun wedding	*eine Mussehe schließen; heiraten müssen*
bad-mouth someone	*schlecht über jemanden reden; Lügen über jemanden verbreiten*

Test your memory: Use the idiom

1. We have to be careful with her. We know she *flings dirt at* everybody.
2. It was all very sudden. *Jim had to get married.* His girl friend got pregnant.
3. I haven't seen you for ages. *Where have you been all this time?*

3. At the party – *Auf der Party*

hold a stag night	*einen Junggesellenabend (Polterabend) veranstalten*
get on the blower to someone	*jemanden anrufen*
be like a cat on hot bricks	*wie eine Katze auf dem heißen Blechdach / sehr nervös sein*

Test your memory: Correct the mistakes

1. Since the new boss arrived Sue has been *like a stag on hot bricks.*
2. When you've collected the necessary information, *get on the mower* to me, will you?
3. Jim *held his cat night* last night. We all got drunk.

Time for a smile

It's hard to feel as fit as a fiddle
when you're shaped like a cello.

B The main COURSE

1. Polite noises – *Höflichkeiten*

Compliments – *Komplimente*

fish for compliments	*auf Komplimente aus sein*
look as if one has just stepped out of a fashion catalogue	*wie aus dem Ei gepellt aussehen*
be the perfect gentleman	*ein Kavalier alter Schule sein*
a touch of perfection	*ein Hauch von Perfektion*
be second to none	*unerreicht sein*
be an artist through and through	*ein Künstler durch und durch sein*
be the life and soul of the company	*die Seele der Firma sein*
be the picture of health	*wie das blühende Leben aussehen*
change for the better	*sich zum Vorteil verändern*
a feather in one's cap	*etwas, worauf man stolz sein kann*
You don't look your age.	*Man sieht Ihnen Ihr Alter nicht an.*
He's your spitting image.	*Er ist Ihnen wie aus dem Gesicht geschnitten.*
Your wish is my command.	*Ihr Wunsch ist mir Befehl.*
You've got to hand it to her – she is extremely clever.	*Das muss man ihr lassen – sie ist sehr schlau.*
He's a man after my own heart.	*Er ist ein Mann so recht nach meinem Geschmack.*
He's enough to make you want to puke. (sl)	*Er ist ein richtiges Brechmittel.*

Time for a smile

Two elderly ladies met at a banquet after an absence of ten years. Said the first, "Good gracious, Elizabeth, I haven't seen you for ages. You certainly look a lot older."
"You look much older too, Dorothy, dear. I wouldn't have recognised you except for the dress and hat."

Congratulations – *Glückwünsche*

wish someone a speedy recovery	*jemandem gute Besserung wünschen*
give someone full marks	*jemandem höchstes Lob spenden*
wish someone all the best	*jemandem das Allerbeste wünschen*
Full marks!	*Perfekt! In allen Punkten bestanden!*
Well done!	*Prima! Klasse! Herzlichen Glück-*
	wunsch!
Great show!	*Toll! Prima!*
Right on target!	*Bingo! Richtig geraten!*
Best / Good wishes to ...	*Die besten Wünsche zu ...*
Bull's eye!	*Volltreffer! Voll ins Schwarze!*
Many happy returns!	*Herzlichen Glückwunsch zum*
	Geburtstag!
Happy New Year!	*Ein frohes neues Jahr!*

Idioms overheard

Two secretaries discuss clothing, Mary (**M**) and Sue (**S**):

S: Anyway I bought this dress yesterday.

M: Well, I have *to hand it to you*. You've got really good dress sense.

S: Oh, I don't know. It's just for the party tomorrow.

M: You'll certainly *be the life and soul of the party* looking like that.

Toasts – *Trinksprüche*

raise one's glass to ...	*auf das Wohl von ... anstoßen*
make a toast to ...	*einen Toast auf ... ausbringen*
propose a toast to ...	*einen Toast auf ... ausbringen*
drink someone's health	*auf jemandes Gesundheit trinken*
drink a toast to someone / something	*auf jemanden / etwas anstoßen*
To your good health!	*Auf Ihr Wohl!*
Here's to the company!	*Auf das Wohl der Firma!*
Bottoms up!	*Ex!; Runter damit!*

Cheers!	*Prost!*
Up yours!	*Hoch die Tassen!*
Well, down the hatch!	*Prost!; Runter damit!*
All the best!	*Alles Gute!*

2. What to small-talk about – *Über was man so redet*

Talking about the weather – *Über das Wetter reden*

suffer a heat spell	*unter einer Hitzewelle leiden*
be boiling hot / be as hot as hell (sl)	*höllisch heiß sein*
have a drought	*eine Dürreperiode haben*
get goose pimples	*eine Gänsehaut bekommen*
be overcast	*bewölkt / zugezogen sein*
be clouded up	*völlig bewölkt sein*
rain cats and dogs	*in Strömen gießen*
bucket down	*wie aus Kübeln gießen*
get / be wet through	*nass bis auf die Haut werden;*
	völlig durchweicht sein
It's brass-monkey weather.	*Es friert Stein und Bein.*
It's weather fit for a duck!	*Es ist ein schönes Sauwetter.*
It's not fit to turn a dog out.	*Bei diesem Wetter jagt man*
	keinen Hund vor die Tür.

 Idioms overheard

Salesman Ron (**R**) and his customer Dave (**D**):

R: What weather you've got up here in the north. *It's not fit to turn a dog out* in.

D: Wait till the hot weather *sets in*. That's the other extreme. We even *had* a sort of *drought* last year.

R: Well, at least, you have a comfortable warm office here. That brings me to our latest catalogue. Would you care to ...?

Everybody's health – *Das werte Befinden*

be fit as a fiddle	*fit wie ein Turnschuh sein*
be coming down with flu	*eine Grippe ausbrüten*
be on one's last legs	*auf dem letzten Loch pfeifen*
be as blind as a bat	*blind wie ein Maulwurf sein*
be in the family way	*in anderen Umständen sein*
be out of the wood(s)	*über den Berg sein*
push up the daisies	*ins Gras beißen*
have one foot in the grave	*mit einem Bein im Grab stehen*
be as dead as a doornail	*mausetot sein*
be as strong as a horse / an ox	*Bärenkräfte haben*

Gossip – *Klatsch*

be fooling around with one's secretary	*etwas mit seiner Sekretärin haben*
turn in one's grave	*sich im Grabe umdrehen*
have a big mouth	*ein vorlautes Mundwerk haben*
set the tongues wagging	*sich die Mäuler zerreißen*
be the talk of the town	*Stadtgespräch sein*
tell tales out of school	*aus der Schule plaudern; tratschen*
a little bird told me ...	*mein kleiner Finger sagt mir ...*
hear it on the grapevine	*gerüchteweise hören*
run down, pull to pieces	*über jemanden herziehen*
fling / throw dirt at someone	*jemanden in den Schmutz ziehen*
get the low-down on someone	*die Wahrheit über jemanden erfahren*
be well-heeled	*gut betucht sein*
let off steam	*Dampf ablassen*
give the shirt off one's back	*sein letztes Hemd geben*
Keep in touch!	*Lass was von dir hören!*
You scratch my back and I'll scratch yours.	*Eine Hand wäscht die andere.*

Idioms overheard

Two clerks, Tony (**T**) and John (**J**), discuss a new law:

T: Have you *got the low-down on* the new law on pseudo-self-employment?

J: Not officially, but I *heard it on the grapevine* that our suppliers will need more than one customer.

T: That'll cause problems. *A little bird told me* that some of our suppliers may just close down. Too much bureaucracy for them.

J: I can believe that.

Wining and Dining – *Fürstlich speisen*

move in the best circles	*sich in den besten Kreisen bewegen*
wine and dine someone	*jemanden fürstlich bewirten*
eat to one's heart's content	*nach Herzenslust essen*
have a sweet tooth	*eine Schwäche für Süßes haben*
have tea and crumpets	*Kaffee und Kuchen zu sich nehmen*
grab / have a bite	*einen Happen essen*
go / be on a diet	*eine Diät machen*
be / go on the wagon	*trocken sein; keinen Alkohol mehr trinken*
be starving to death	*fast verhungert sein*
fced one's face (sl)	*sich den Bauch voll schlagen*
have a square meal	*eine kräftige Mahlzeit zu sich nehmen*
That'll stick to your ribs.	*Das wird dich satt machen.*
eat high on the hog	*gierig verschlingen*
That makes my mouth water.	*Da läuft einem das Wasser im Mund zusammen.*
Dig into the food! (informal)	*Greift zu! Lasst es euch schmecken!*
Come and get it!	*Essen ist fertig! Kommt alle zum Essen!*
eat one's fill	*sich satt essen*
drink one's fill	*dem Wein ausgiebig zusprechen*
have a drop too much	*zu tief ins Glas schauen*
wet one's whistle	*sich die Kehle anfeuchten*
spend a night on the tiles	*die ganze Nacht durchzechen*
paint the town red	*auf Zechtour gehen*
pick up the tab / foot the bill	*die Zeche zahlen*

Idioms overheard

A young couple, Sally (**S**) and Mick (**M**):

M: It's great to *eat out* together again, isn't it?

S: Yes, and that swordfish is *making my mouth water*.

M: Hmmm, it's a bit expensive, though.

S: Don't worry about that. We can *go dutch*. Remember, I've got a new job now.

3. At the party – *Auf der Party*

throw a housewarming party	*eine Einweihungsparty schmeißen*
invite to a stag party	*zu einem Polterabend (des Bräutigams) einladen*
organise a hen-party	*einen Polterabend (für die Braut) organisieren*
be in full swing	*in vollem Gange sein*
drop by / in	*vorbei-/ hereinschauen*
put in an appearance	*sich blicken lassen; auf der Bildfläche erscheinen*
break the ice	*das Eis brechen*
be the life and soul of the party	*Alleinunterhalter der Party sein*
be a wallflower	*Mauerblümchen sein*
welcome someone with open arms	*jemanden mit offenen Armen willkommen heißen*
have the time of one's life	*sich königlich amüsieren*
be bored out of one's mind	*sich zu Tode langweilen*
let one's hair down	*sich ungeniert benehmen*
rub shoulders with vips	*mit Promis auf du und du sein*
go to the john / gents / restroom / lavatory	*auf die Toilette gehen*
see a man about a dog	*das Klo aufsuchen*

Idioms overheard

Tom (**T**) and Bob (**B**) at the office party:

B: I was really annoyed that I had to work overtime on Saturday last week.

T: It's passed. *It's no good crying over spilt milk.*

B: Well, my girlfriend broke off our relationship because of that.

T: Don't worry! Come to my party and I promise *you won't be a wall-flower.*

C Idioms AT WORK

TASK 1: Do you remember?

Translate the phrases in brackets.

1. We've had flooding all week and it's still (*regnen wie aus Kübeln*)
2. The files for the seminar *got* (*völlig durchweicht*) in the rain.
3. Anne's so sensitive. She's got (*Gänsehaut*) three quarters of the year.

TASK 2: Idioms for alcoholics

1. I know it's early, but I'll *wet my* _____ in any case. I'm thirsty.
2. Tom got a headache. I guess he had *a* _____ *too much* last night.
3. We've won the lottery. Let's go out and _____ *the town red*.

TASK 3: What do you say?

1. It's your uncle's birthday.   "_____!"
2. You meet the boss on January 1st.   "_____!"
3. You visit Tom in hospital.   "_____!"
4. You raise your glass of champagne.   "_____!"

149

TASK 4: Incompatible characters

Two sisters, Milly and Olga, are discussing their friend Tina.
Olga is contradicting Milly. Complete her idioms.

M: Doesn't Tina *look the picture of health*?

O: I think she *looks* rather *like* _____ warmed _____.

M: Tom, her fiancé, is *a man after my own heart.*

O: What? He's *enough to make me want to* _____.

M: She's invited me to her *stag party.*

O: *Stag party*? You mean '_____ party'.

M: You're invited, too. Why don't you join us? You'll *be the life and soul of the party.*

O: I hate parties. I'm the born _____.

M: Come on! I'm sure you'd *have the time of your life.*

O: Nonsense! I'd *be* _____ ___ *of my mind.*

TASK 5: Tim, the 'Yes-man'

Help Tim to echo what Tom has said.

1

Tom: Look, there's young Freddy Flinton. Isn't he his father's spitting image? And he's got his father's bad character, too.

Tim: Yes, *he's a* _____ *off the old* _____.

2

Tom: His father forced him to marry Susan Smith. He got her pregnant.

Tim: Yes, it was *a* _____-_____ *marriage.*

3

Tom: The whole neighbourhood is talking about nothing else.

Tim: Yes, this marriage has set *a lot of* _____ *wagging.* It's the *talk of the* _____.

4

Tom: Old Maggie has been saying very unpleasant things about Freddy Flinton.

Tim: Yes, she's _____ *dirt at Freddy.*

5

Tom: She should be careful. Old Flinton can be very nasty and he has friends at the Town Hall.

Tim: Yes, he _____ *shoulders* with important people at the Town Hall.

TASK 6: Magic squares – The animal world

Match the phrases (1, 2, 3) with the words in the box (A, B, C). Put the numbers in the magic squares. Columns and rows will all add up to the same number, **15**.

A. dog	D. monkey	G. hen
B. bird's	E. stag	H. duck
C. goose	F. cats	I. bat

1. It's weather fit for a ★.
2. What weather! It's not fit to turn a ★ out.
3. What a country! It's raining ★ and dogs again.
4. What a summer! Look, I've even got get ★ pimples.
5. Has Tom invited you to his ★ -party, too?
6. I think I'll go to Milly's ★-party.
7. What a climate! It's brass- ★ weather again.
8. I can't see anything. I'm as blind as a ★.
9. On the first page of each module we give you a ★-eye view of the content.

A =	B =	C =
D =	E =	F =
G =	H =	I =

Did you know these animals?
goose (geese pl): *Gans*; stag: *Hirsch*; duck: *Ente*; bat: *Fledermaus*

EXCHANGE OF ARGUMENTS
AUSTAUSCH VON ARGUMENTEN

Discussion, whether it is an everyday topic or in a specialist negotiation, can become a delicate matter. Indeed it can be a time-bomb resulting in an explosion, after which discussion partners end up not speaking to each other, at all. Discussion involves giving opinions, agreeing, disagreeing, and generally being a clever tactician. And most important, talkers should be good listeners and fair-minded so that they can appreciate the opinions[1] of others.

Bird's eye view

1. Giving one's opinion	*Seine Meinung äußern*
2. Changing one's opinion	*Seine Meinung ändern*
3. Taking a stand	*Stellung beziehen*
4. The bad tactician	*Der schlechte Taktiker*
5. Disagreeing	*Anderer Meinung sein*
6. Agreeing	*Einer Meinung sein*

Time for a smile

The other day my boss told me that he'd welcome an exchange of opinions. What he meant by that is that I should come with my opinion and walk away with his.

A business phrase to remember:
1 appreciate someone's opinions: *jemandes Meinung zu schätzen wissen*

A   A FIRST TASTE of idioms

1. Giving one's opinion – *Seine Meinung äußern*

make no bones about	*nicht lange fackeln; nicht viel Federlesens machen*
speak up	*frei heraus sprechen*
give someone a piece of one's mind	*jemandem deutlich die Meinung sagen*

Test your memory: Compare and correct the mistakes

1. He's wasted hundreds of pounds. I'll give him a *peace of my mind* when I see him.
2. I'll *make no bones of* it. We're in real trouble.
3. *Speak up*, man! I need your opinion about it.

2. Changing one's opinion – *Seine Meinung ändern*

change one's tune	*neue Töne von sich geben*
move the goal posts	*die Spielregeln ändern*
try another tack	*den Kurs wechseln*

Test your memory: What's the *woggle*?

1. This meeting has come to a standstill. Let's try another *woggle*.
2. We agreed there would be no public criticism. You're moving the goal *woggles* with this dirty trick.
3. You want to live abroad. My goodness, you've *woggled* your tune.

Time for a smile

"I don't like 'yes-men' around me," said the boss to the new employee. "When I say 'No', I want them to say 'No', too."

3. Taking a stand – *Stellung beziehen*

be the last resort	*die letzte Zuflucht sein*
drive something home	*etwas klar machen; etwas nach-* *drücklich vor Augen führen*
show one's true colours	*Farbe bekennen*

Test your memory

1. The crisis has _____ home to the board the need for a change in policy.
2. Firing the man is only the last _____. Let's discuss it.
3. Once he achieved power he showed his true _____.

4. The bad tactician – *Der schlechte Taktiker*

miss the point	*das Wesentliche nicht begreifen*
see everything black and white	*alles nur schwarzweiß sehen*
flog a dead horse	*offene Türen einrennen*

Test your memory: Compare and correct

1. Be more flexible. You see everything so *dead and white*.
2. Forget it! It's no use. You're missing a *black horse*.
3. You didn't get it. You've *flogged the point*.

Time for a smile

"Dobson," said the boss one morning, "I just don't know how we are going to get along without you – but starting Monday, we're going to try."

5. Disagreeing – *Anderer Meinung sein*

beg to differ	*bitten, anderer Meinung sein zu dürfen*
have other fish to fry	*Wichtigeres zu tun haben*
go against the grain	*gegen den Strich gehen*

Test your memory: Use the idioms

1. We haven't got the time. We *have more important business to do.*
2. We heard what you said but unfortunately I must say I *don't agree.*
3. It *is really a damned nuisance* to have to go into the office at weekends.

6. Agreeing – *Gleicher Meinung sein*

just the ticket	*genau das Richtige*
join the club	*ganz Ihrer Meinung*
be just the job	*gerade das Richtige sein*

Test your memory: Use the idioms

1. A house in Spain, good food and wine. That's just *what I need.*
2. I hate this climate. – Well, *so do I.*
3. Buy a new house and save £50,000? That's just we were waiting for.

Time for a smile

The company has been expanding on the home market[1], so the boss invited his sales team into his office. "You have done so well that I'm giving you each a cheque for $1,500," he said – and on second thoughts – he added, "and if you keep on working like this, I might even sign them."

....

A business phrase to remember:
1 expand on the home market: *auf dem Binnenmarkt expandieren*

B   The main COURSE

1. Giving one's opinion – *Seine Meinung äußern*

know one's own mind	*genau wissen, was man will*
get something off one's mind	*sich etwas von der Seele reden*
to my way of thinking	*meiner Meinung nach*
take the view that	*die Ansicht vertreten, dass*
air one's opinion	*seine Meinung darlegen*
stick to one's guns	*auf seinem Standpunkt beharren*
have one's say	*seine Meinung äußern*
say one's piece	*sagen, was man zu sagen hat*
make one's point	*sein Argument vorbringen*
put / set the record straight	*etwas klarstellen / ins rechte Licht rücken*
make no bones about	*nicht viel Federlesens machen*
not pull one's punches	*kein Blatt vor den Mund nehmen*
speak one's mind in no uncertain terms	*seine Meinung klipp und klar sagen*
not mince one's words	*kein Blatt vor den Mund nehmen*
put one's two cents (worth) in	*seinen Senf dazugeben*
take a firm stand	*einen festen Standpunkt beziehen*

Idioms overheard

Negotiations about selling Comby GmbH to Unlingua.
Ron (**R**) of Comby, Shark (**S**) of Unlingua:

S: Just *to put the record straight*, we can only offer you DM 700,000 and not DM 900,000 as you wanted.

R: Then I'm afraid it's no go. I'm *sticking to my guns* on this one.

S: Look, *I'm not going to mince words with you*. You won't get a better offer. Not for the Heidelberg district.

R: Well, *to my way of thinking* it's got to be in your interests to get in here.

2. Changing one's opinion – *Seine Meinung ändern*

change one's tune	*seine Meinung ändern; umschwenken; neue Töne von sich geben*
shift one's ground	*seine Haltung / Einstellung ändern*
on the wrong track	*auf dem Holzweg*
turn it over in one's mind	*sich etwas durch den Kopf gehen lassen*
try / take another tack	*es anders versuchen*
blow hot and cold	*sich mal so und mal so entscheiden*
be in two minds about	*sich nicht entscheiden können; hin- und hergerissen sein*
be torn between two possibilities	*zwischen zwei Möglichkeiten hin- und hergerissen sein*
cloud the issue	*den Sachverhalt vernebeln*
be caught between the devil and the deep blue sea	*in einer Zwickmühle stecken*
be in a catch 22 situation	*in einem Dilemma sein; in einem Teufelskreis stecken*
jump out of the frying pan into the fire	*vom Regen in die Traufe kommen*

 ### Idioms overheard

Two sales managers discuss a strategy, Rick (**R**) and Dave (**D**):

R: We won't win. *It's a catch twenty-two situation.* If we set up an agency, we have high costs. We can't afford it[1].

D: And if we don't, we lose the market there and we can't afford that either.

R: And if, by any chance, we don't get more customers through the agency, we'll be jumping *out of the frying pan into the fire.*

D: I know what you mean. I'm *blowing hot and cold on this one.*

....

A business phrase to remember:
1 we can't afford it: *wir können es uns nicht leisten*

3. Taking a stand – *Stellung beziehen*

make a stand against	*Stellung beziehen / Front machen gegen*
nail someone down to something	*jemanden auf etwas festnageln*
nail one's colours to the mast	*Farbe bekennen; Flagge zeigen*
show one's hand	*mit offenen Karten spielen*
show one's true colours	*sein wahres Gesicht zeigen*
put one's finger on something	*den Finger auf etwas legen*
call a spade a spade	*die Dinge beim Namen nennen*
get to the heart of the matter	*zum Kern der Sache kommen*
put two and two together	*sich etwas zusammenreimen*
weigh up the pros and cons	*das Für und Wider abwägen*
bring to a head / climax	*auf die Spitze treiben*
drive someone into a corner	*jemanden in die Ecke drängen*
pick holes in an argument	*ein Argument entkräften*
turn the tables	*den Spieß umdrehen*
read someone's thoughts / mind	*jemandes Gedanken lesen*
lay a trap	*eine Falle stellen*
drive something home	*etwas klar machen; etwas nachdrücklich vor Augen führen*
steamroller someone	*jemanden überrollen*
catch someone off guard / unawares / on the wrong foot	*jemanden auf dem falschen Fuß erwischen*
get off on the right foot	*einen guten Anfang machen*
pull something to pieces	*kein gutes Haar an etwas lassen*
open someone's eyes	*jemandem die Augen öffnen*
sound someone out	*jemanden aushorchen*

Idioms overheard

A problem of personnel, Rutert (**R**), Tissmann (**T**):

R: We shouldn't let personal feelings *cloud the issue*. He's not done his work properly, he hasn't performed[1].

T: You must have been *reading my mind*. But it's a difficult situation. We don't want *to steamroller* him.

R: Look, there's no way out. I like *to call a spade a spade*.

....

A business phrase to remember: 1 he hasn't performed: *er hat nichts geleistet*

4. The bad tactician – *Der schlechte Taktiker*

be slow on the uptake	*eine lange Leitung haben*
join the other side	*die Fronten wechseln*
beat about the bush	*um den heißen Brei herumreden*
be on shaky ground	*auf tönernen Füßen stehen*
be on a knife-edge about something	*wegen etwas auf glühenden Kohlen sitzen*
beg the question	*Antwort auf eine Frage schuldig bleiben*
rush headlong into something	*sich Hals über Kopf in etwas stürzen*
get out of / go beyond one's depth	*den sicheren Boden unter den Füßen verlassen*
miss the point	*nicht verstehen, um was es geht*
get hold of the wrong end of the stick	*etwas in den falschen Hals kriegen*
not see the wood for the trees	*den Wald vor lauter Bäumen nicht sehen*
burn one's boats / bridges	*alle Brücken hinter sich abbrechen*
I've reached the point of no return.	*Es gibt für mich kein Zurück mehr.*
bury one's head in the sand	*Vogel-Strauß-Politik betreiben*
read something into somebody's words	*etwas in jemandes Worte hineinlegen*
bark up the wrong tree	*auf der falschen Fährte / dem Holzweg sein*
not have a leg to stand on	*seine Behauptungen nicht beweisen können; nichts in der Hand haben*
cut off one's nose to spite one's face	*sich ins eigene Fleisch schneiden*
saw off the branch one is sitting on	*den Ast absägen, auf dem man sitzt*
dig one's own grave	*sein eigenes Grab schaufeln*

Idioms overheard

The salary talk. Employee (**E**), department leader (**L**):

E: So I think I should have a rise[1] of DM 500 per month.

L: I'm afraid you're *barking up the wrong tree*. There's nothing left in the budget here.

E: I think you *are on shaky ground* there. I know we make a large profit and my work was good.

L: I don't know where you got your information, but you've *read something into* it which wasn't there.

5. Disagreeing – *Anderer Meinung sein*

be at loggerheads	*verschiedener Meinung sein; uneins sein*
not in a month of Sundays!	*kommt gar nicht in die Tüte*
upset the applecart	*die Pläne durchkreuzen*
not do something for all the tea in China	*etwas nicht um alles in der Welt tun*
be out of the question	*gar nicht in Frage kommen; unmöglich sein*
be out of tune with someone	*mit jemandem nicht harmonieren*
One man's meat is another man's poison.	*Des einen Freud ist des anderen Leid.*
take exception to something	*gegen etwas protestieren*
leave someone out on a limb	*jemanden im Regen stehen lassen*
not see eye-to-eye with someone	*nicht mit jemandem übereinstimmen*
agree to differ	*jedem das Recht auf seine Meinung zugestehen*

A business phrase to remember:
1 I should have a rise: *ich sollte eine Gehaltserhöhung bekommen*

Idioms overheard

In a company, personnel manager (**M**) and employee (**E**):

M: So we'd like to transfer[1] you to our agency in Libya.

E: I wouldn't go there *in a month of Sundays*. That's in the middle of nowhere.

M: But it's still a job. *You're on the wrong track* if you think you can work where you want.

E: In any case, I absolutely *take exception to* that idea.

6. Agreeing – *Einer Meinung sein*

get the message	*die Botschaft verstehen; etwas kapieren*
take the point	*verstehen, was jemand meint*
back someone's schemes / ideas	*jemandes Pläne / Ideen unterstützen*
be in line with	*übereinstimmen mit*
fit into the picture	*in das Bild passen*
that's right up / down my alley / street	*das ist genau mein Fall; das ist was für mich*
go fifty-fifty; go halves	*halbe-halbe machen*
reach an understanding	*zu einer Einigung gelangen*
put one's heads together	*etwas gemeinsam besprechen*
Join the club!	*Ganz Ihrer Meinung!*
fit (or fill) the bill	*den Erwartungen entsprechen; den Anforderungen genügen*
just what the doctor ordered; just the job; just the ticket	*genau das Richtige; genau das, was man sich wünscht*
eat out of the palm of someone's hand	*jemandem aus der Hand fressen*
be fine and dandy	*alles bestens sein*
shake hands on something	*durch Handschlag bekräftigen*

(siehe auch Module 8: Negotiating)

A business phrase to remember:
1 transfer someone: *jemanden versetzen*

Idioms overheard

A happy conclusion. Andrew (**A**), sales manager from P & O, Jenny (**J**) from Office Accessories:

J: Well, your transportation schedule exactly *fits the bill*. As far as we're concerned it's *just the ticket:* price and schedule are fair enough.

A: Customisation, *that's right up our street*. I'm glad we could satisfy you. *Let's shake hands* on it, shall we?

J: Here's my hand.

Time for a smile

One day McGrub, boss of a large clothing store, said to his new assistant, "I'll be away on business tomorrow, John, and I'm going to set you a real test of your abilities. I want you to get rid of that terrible yellow jacket with the green trousers. We've had it on the rack for two years."

When the boss returned he asked the assistant if he had managed to sell the suit. "Oh, yes. I sold it for £300."

"Excellent," said the boss. "Did you have a hard time selling it?" – "Not really," replied the assistant. "I had no trouble with the customer, but I did have a hell of an argument with his guide-dog."

C   Idioms AT WORK

TASK 1:   Odd man out

Which idiom has a completely different meaning? Translate it.

1. Our director speaks his mind in no uncertain terms.
   A. Yes, he doesn't pull his punches.
   B. Yes, he doesn't mince his word.
   C. Yes, he doesn't stick to his guns.

2. Has he made up his mind about firing his junior partner?
   A. No, he's still in two minds.
   B. No, he's still caught between the devil and the deep blue sea.
   C. No, he's still be torn between two possibilities.

3. I think by firing his junior partner he might be cutting his own throat.
   A. Yes, he might be on shaky ground.
   B. Yes, he might be digging his own grave.
   C. Yes, he might be sawing off the branch he's sitting on.

TASK 2:   Why Tim will not climb the ladder

All the things you need are made of wood.

1. He often misunderstands. He's always *barking up the wrong* _____.
2. And as soon as he has found the right tree *he saws off the branch he's* _____ *on.*
3. In meetings he always *gets hold of the wrong end of the* _____.
4. He's thinking about resigning -if he resigns *he will have burnt his* _____ and he might regret it.
5. Tim *cannot see the* _____ *for the* _____.

Food for thought

Tell your boss what you really think of him
and the truth will set you free. *Patrick Murray*

TASK 3: "Metallic" idioms

All the things you need are made of metal.

1. He refused to change his strategy in spite of criticism. *He stuck to his* _____.

2. He's a real bore at meetings. He's always *putting his two* _____ *in.*

3. Did you pass your exam? – No idea, *I'm on a* _____ about the results.

4. He left Russia and immigrated to Israel, and that *was jumping out of the frying-* _____ *into the fire.*

TASK 4: Time for a rhyme

Find the rhyme.

Caught between the devil and the deep blue _____?
No! I think you're barking up the wrong _____.
Don't bury your head in the _____.
Roll up your sleeves and take a _____
Take stock, change track and _____.
Louder than words speak actions.
Wake up and make decisions.
Weigh up the pros and ____.
And stick to your _____,
My son!

TASK 5: Tim, the 'Yes-man'

1

Tom: These journalists are writing a lot of lies about our new pill Shot. We should *publish a correct version of facts.*

Tim: Yes, let's release a press statement to *put the record* _____.

2

Tom: We must *make them understand* that Shot has no side effects.

Tim: Yes, we must *drive that message* _____.

3

Tom: They *have nothing to support the claim* that Shot causes impotence.

Tim: Right, they *haven't a* _____ *to stand on.*

4

Tom: And write a letter of complaint to the editor of this paper.
And *don't mince your words.*

Tim: Yes, I certainly won't *pull my* _____.

5

Tom: We'll *declare publicly and firmly* that we won't take Shot off the
market just because some old spinsters feel sexually inadequate.

Tim: Yes, *let's* _____ *our* _____ *to the mast.*

TASK 6:	Remember our business phrases?

1. jemandes Meinung zu schätzen wissen   _____
2. auf dem Binnenmarkt expandieren   _____
3. er hat nichts geleistet   _____
4. ich sollte eine Gehaltserhöhung bekommen   _____
5. jemanden nach Libyen versetzen   _____

TASK 7:	Do you remember the German?

Caught between the devil and the deep blue *sea?*

_____

I think you're barking up the wrong *tree.*

_____

Don't bury your head in the *sand.*

_____

Roll up your sleeves and take a *stand.*

_____

Weigh up the pros and *cons.*

_____

And stick to your *guns.*

PRAISING AND CRITICISING
LOBEN UND KRITISIEREN

All of us make mistakes and when we are found out we can expect criticism. Sometimes it's fair, sometimes not, but it'll be there in any case. We have to learn how to manage it. To see it positively, if we don't have criticism or feedback we have no chance to improve what we do. We shouldn't allow our feelings to get involved.

Bird's eye view

1. Human weaknesses	*Menschliche Schwächen*
2. Mild and harsh criticism	*Milde und scharfe Kritik*
3. Showing understanding	*Verständnis zeigen*
4. Praising someone	*Jemanden loben*
5. Reasons for praising	*Gründe für Lob*

Time for a smile

"Congratulations, my boy," said the father of the bride. "I'm sure you will look back on today as the happiest day of your life."
"But we aren't not getting married until tomorrow," protested the lad.
"I know," said the father.

A   A FIRST TASTE of idioms

1. Human weaknesses – *Menschliche Schwächen*

beef about something	*über etwas meckern*
jump the gun	*voreilig sein*
be at sixes and sevens	*drunter und drüber gehen*

Test your memory: Correct the mistakes

1. Don't *gun the jump*! Wait till he makes his offer.
2. Bob's always *eating about* something. He's never satisfied.
3. Our management style is *at sevens and sixes*. No logic at all.

2. Mild and harsh criticism – *Milde und scharfe Kritik*

tick someone off	*jemandem einen Rüffel geben*
give someone what for	*jemanden abkanzeln*
send someone packing	*jemanden rausschmeißen*

Test your memory: There are several words too many.
Cross them out.

1. He's made a fool of us. I'll *give him what he came for* when he comes.
2. Every time you make a mistake, the boss will *tick you off the pay list*.
3. As soon as we'd found out what he'd done we *sent him packing his suitcases*.

> ### Time for a smile
>
> Guide on a conducted tour of Rome: "And this ancient monument dates back over 2500 years." – "Don't be ridiculous," said one little old lady. "It's only 2002 now ..."

3. Showing understanding – *Verständnis zeigen*

not to be too hard on someone	*jemanden nicht zu hart anfassen*
be big of someone	*sehr nett von jemandem sein*
make allowances for someone	*jemanden mit Nachsicht behandeln*

Test your memory: Wrong order – letters are at six and sevens. Can you fix them?

1. We've *to make wallsonace* for the new teacher. He's in a wheelchair.
2. Don't *be too drah on* him. It's his first job.
3. That's *gib of you to* offer to pay, but we don't need it.

4. Praising someone – *Jemanden loben*

sing someone's praises	*einen Lobgesang auf jemanden anstimmen*
give someone his due	*jemandem Gerechtigkeit widerfahren lassen*
have to hand it to someone	*jemandem etwas lassen müssen*

Test your memory

1. I don't like him personally, but *give him his* _____, he got very good results.
2. He's *singing his secretary's* _____ all the time. I wonder why.
3. You *have to* _____ *it to* her. She's a top-class athlete.

Time for a smile

Fred is darn lucky. He has got a wife and a transistor – and they both work.

5. Reasons for praising – *Gründe für Lob*

bear fruit	*Früchte tragen*
be a sight for sore eyes	*ein erfreulicher Anblick sein*
put on a brave face	*gute Miene zum bösen Spiel machen*

Test your memory: Let's go *woggling* again

1. His company went bankrupt. Nevertheless he's managing to *woggle on a brave woggle*.
2. There's nothing but trouble here. But you're *a woggle for sore woggles*. Thank God you've arrived.
3. Our investments are beginning to *bear woggle*.

A   The main COURSE

1. Human weaknesses – *Menschliche Schwächen*

Mental qualities

He's not exactly an Einstein.	*Er hat das Pulver nicht erfunden.*
There's one born every minute.	*Die Dummen werden nicht alle.*
be slow on the uptake	*schwer von Begriff sein*
be as thick as two short planks / a brick (sl)	*dumm wie Bohnenstroh sein*
be a bit dim	*die Weisheit nicht gerade mit Löffeln gefressen haben*
have a memory / head like a sieve	*ein Gedächtnis wie ein Sieb haben*
not achieve anything to write home about	*nichts erreichen, was der Rede wert ist*
have a screw loose	*eine Schraube locker haben*
have a bee in one's bonnet	*eine fixe Idee haben*

have a one-track mind	*nur eingleisig denken können*
build castles in the air	*Luftschlösser bauen*
live in cloud cuckoo land	*im Wolkenkuckucksheim leben*
live in a fool's paradise	*sich Illusionen machen*
chase after rainbows	*Illusionen nachjagen*

About employees and colleagues

be a son of a bitch	*ein Miststück sein*
be a so-and-so	*ein blöder Hund sein*
be a glutton for punishment	*nach Bestrafung geradezu schreien*
He's a dead loss.	*Er ist ein hoffnungsloser Fall.*
He's a turkey [US].	*Er ist ein totaler Versager.*
It's like teaching your grandmother to suck eggs.	*Da will das Ei wieder klüger sein als die Henne.*
a loose cannon	*ein Unsicherheitsfaktor / unberechenbar sein*
be a stick in the mud	*eine lahme Ente sein*
be a millstone round someone's neck	*ein Klotz am Bein sein*
be a square peg in a round hole	*ein Mensch am falschen Platz sein*
be a lazy bones	*ein Faulpelz sein*
He's at sixes and sevens.	*Bei ihm geht alles drunter und drüber.*
make a real howler	*einen Bock schießen*
be all fingers and thumbs	*zwei linke Hände haben*
fail / flunk one's exam	*im Examen durchfallen*
bite off more than one can chew	*sich überschätzen*
be a copycat	*ein Nachahmer sein*
not be able / not fit to hold a candle to someone	*jemandem das Wasser nicht reichen können*
not be in the same league as someone	*sich mit jemandem nicht messen können*
not to be a patch on someone	*sich nicht mit jemandem vergleichen können*
not be able to touch someone	*jemandem das Wasser nicht reichen können*
be a size too small for	*eine Nummer zu klein sein für*

step out of line	*sich nicht an die Regeln halten*
be moaning and groaning all the time.	*fortwährend jammern*
pass the buck to someone	*jemandem den schwarzen Peter zuschieben*
take the easy way out	*es sich leicht machen*
be a good-for-nothing	*ein Nichtsnutz sein*
be a wet blanket	*ein Spielverderber / Störenfried sein*
be a doubting Thomas	*ein ungläubiger Thomas sein*
be a jack-of-all-trades	*ein Hansdampf in allen Gassen sein*
be a cold fish	*ein eiskalter Hund sein*
be the black sheep	*das schwarze Schaf sein*
behave like a bull in a china shop	*sich wie ein Elefant im Porzellanladen benehmen*
rock the boat	*Wellen machen; die Sache gefährden*
be a fuss-pot	*ein Umstandskrämer sein*
Give him an inch and he'll takes a mile.	*Wenn man ihm den kleinen Finger reicht, nimmt er die ganze Hand.*
lie through one's teeth	*lügen wie gedruckt*
be a hard nut to crack	*ein harte Nuss sein*

 Idioms overheard

Two colleagues, Rob (**R**) and Dave (**D**), are discussing their new boss:

R: What about our new man at the top?

D: In a way he is behaving *like a bull in a china shop*. He's very heavy-handed.

R: I guess you're right. You shouldn't give him too much information. *Give him an inch and he'll take a mile.*

D: Well, it's no good *us moaning and groaning all the time.* We've got to work with him in any case.

2. Mild and harsh criticism – *Milde und scharfe Kritik*

be a queer bird	*ein komischer Vogel*
handle someone with kid gloves	*jemanden mit Samthandschuhen anfassen*
damn with faint praise	*durch die Blume kritisieren*
raise one's eyebrows at something	*die Stirn wegen etwas runzeln*
pull one's punches	*sich mit Kritik zurückhalten*
find fault with someone	*etwas an jemandem auszusetzen haben*
pick away at someone	*an jemandem rumnörgeln*
have a bone to pick with someone	*mit jemandem ein Hühnchen zu rupfen haben*
hold (it) against someone	*jemandem etwas ankreiden*
take someone to task	*sich jemanden vorknöpfen*
tell some home truths	*unbequeme Wahrheiten sagen*
give someone a rap on / over the knuckles	*jemandem auf die Finger klopfen*
take the rap for something	*etwas ausbaden / den Kopf für etwas hinhalten müssen*
get it in the neck	*eins aufs Dach bekommen*
dress someone down	*jemanden abkanzeln*
give someone a dressing-down	*jemandem eins auf den Deckel geben*
bring someone to his senses	*jemanden zur Vernunft bringen*
take someone down a notch / peg (or two)	*jemandem einen Dämpfer aufsetzen; ihn in die Schranken weisen*
cut someone down to size	*jemanden zurechtstutzen; jemandem einen Dämpfer versetzen*
get up someone's nose	*jemandem auf den Geist gehen*
send someone about their business	*jemandem heimleuchten*
tell someone where to get off	*jemandem zeigen, wo es langgeht*
give someone a ticking-off	*jemandem eine Standpauke halten*
read someone the riot act	*jemandem die Leviten lesen*
give someone a real earful	*jemandem eine Standpauke halten*
throw the book at someone	*jemandem die Leviten lesen*
give someone hell	*jemandem die Hölle heiß machen*

make no bones	*nicht viel Federlesens machen*
give someone a rough ride	*jemanden in die Mangel nehmen*
pin someone's ears back	*jemandem eine Abreibung verpassen*
bite someone's head off	*jemandem den Kopf abreißen*
jump down someone's throat	*jemanden anschnauzen*
carpet someone / give someone a carpeting	*jemanden zusammenstauchen*
tear a strip off someone	*jemanden zur Minna machen*
run someone down	*jemanden madig machen*
give someone some flak	*jemanden schwer unter Beschuss nehmen*
rub salt in someone's wounds	*jemandem Salz in die Wunden streuen*
haul someone over the coals	*jemanden fertig machen*
Get your act together.	*Reiß dich zusammen.*
You can put that in your pipe and smoke it!	*Lass dir das gesagt sein!; Schreib dir das hinter die Ohren!*
That will make the feathers fly.	*Da werden die Fetzen fliegen.*
Beggars can't be choosers.	*Arme Leute dürfen nicht wählerisch sein.*
When the cat's away the mice will play.	*Wenn die Katze aus dem Haus ist, tanzen die Mäuse.*

 Idioms overheard

The secretary of the big boss has just been disciplined. He really *gave her a rap on the knuckles*. She had forgotten to send off an important letter to a customer and the boss *made no bones about* the fact that if it happened again she'd be out of a job. He *gave her a real carpeting*, so it must have been something important. But to tell the truth it wasn't the first time she'd *stepped out of line*.

3. Showing understanding – *Verständnis zeigen*

put in a good word for someone	*ein gutes Wort für jemanden einlegen*
give someone the benefit of the doubt	*im Zweifel für den Angeklagten entscheiden*
boost someone's courage	*jemandem Mut machen*
make allowances for	*mit Nachsicht behandeln*
take mitigating circumstances into account	*mildernde Umstände berücksichtigen*
grin and bear it	*gute Miene zum bösen Spiel machen*
turn a blind eye to	*ein Auge zudrücken; etwas absichtlich übersehen*
show understanding for	*Verständnis zeigen für*
be big of someone	*sehr nett / freundlich von jemandem sein*
keep a stiff upper lip	*Haltung bewahren*
stay on the straight and narrow	*auf dem Pfad der Tugend bleiben*
mend one's ways	*sich bessern*
Hold your horses!	*Nicht so stürmisch!; Immer langsam mit den jungen Pferden!*
People in glass houses shouldn't throw stones.	*Wer im Glashaus sitzt, sollte nicht mit Steinen werfen.*
All work and no play makes Jack a dull boy.	*Zu viel Arbeit macht krank.*
hold someone up as an example	*jemanden als leuchtendes Beispiel vorhalten*

 Idioms overheard

When work is stress

We've just gained important new customers, but we have to *handle them with kid gloves*. We're expected to *show understanding* for their difficulties. On the other hand we're not allowed to have an opinion. We're only a supplier and we have to *stay on the straight and narrow*. We shouldn't criticise or else they might sink us. That's business.

4. Praising someone – *Jemanden loben*

take a leaf out of someone's book	*sich an jemandem ein Beispiel nehmen*
give someone a pat on the back	*jemandem anerkennend auf die Schulter klopfen*
sing someone's praises	*einen Lobgesang auf jemanden anstimmen*
praise to the skies	*in den Himmel / über den grünen Klee loben*
go down in history (in the records)	*in die Geschichte eingehen; Geschichte machen*
give someone the red carpet treatment	*den roten Teppich für jemanden ausrollen*
speak highly of someone	*von jemandem in den höchsten Tönen sprechen*
take one's hat off to someone	*vor jemandem den Hut ziehen*
hand it to someone	*jemandem etwas lassen*
go to someone's head	*jemandem zu Kopf steigen*
do someone's heart good	*jemandem gut tun*
Credit where credit's due.	*Ehre, wem Ehre gebührt.*

 Idioms overheard

Look at my department

Everything is *in apple-pie order*. There are no hidden surprises here. We're so successful that I think it's beginning to *go to my head*. Anyway, even with this success nobody is going to *give me the red carpet treatment*. I can forget that.

5. Reasons for praising – *Gründe für Lob*

be in apple-pie order	*picobello / tadellos sein*
be spick and span	*blitzblank / sauber / gepflegt sein*
be as clean as a whistle	*sauber / wie geleckt / blitzeblank sein*
be a high-flyer	*ein Überflieger sein*

be the salt of the earth	*das Salz der Erde sein*
be the apple in someone's eye	*jemandes Augapfel sein*
be an ace	*ein Ass sein*
be one in a thousand	*etwas ganz Besonderes / einzigartig sein*
put on a bold front	*mit Fassung tragen; Haltung bewahren*
put a brave face on something	*gute Miene zum bösen Spiel machen; etwas mit Fassung tragen*
keep a level head	*einen klaren Kopf behalten*
fight to the bitter end	*bis zum bitteren Ende kämpfen*
have the courage of one's convictions	*zu seinen Überzeugungen stehen; Zivilcourage haben*
(be) a feather in one's cap	*auf etwas stolz sein*
have a piece of the action	*seinen Anteil / einen Teil vom Kuchen haben*
work wonders	*wahre Wunder bewirken*
pluck up one's courage	*Mut fassen; seinen ganzen Mut zusammennehmen*
keep one's chin up	*die Ohren steif halten*
You've got to hand it to him!	*Das muss man ihm lassen.*

Idioms overheard

A staff dialogue with a real potential between the department leader (**D**) and an employee (**E**):

D: Well, your work in the last year has shown that you're really *one in a thousand*.

E: Thank you very much. I didn't expect that. All I wanted was a bit of the action in the department.

D: Well, you've done well, but we've a lot of challenges in front of us. So you have to *keep a level head*. Remember, when other members of the department are trying to stick a knife in your back, *have the courage of your convictions*, even if they are all against you.

C   Idioms AT WORK

TASK 1:   Dynamic verbs of movement

Put the verbs into the right gaps. Mind the verb forms.

chase	rock	throw
run	tear	haul
boost	turn	catch

1. Things are progressing well – please don't do anything to _____ the boat.
2. I was _____ over the coals by my boss for being late.
3. The unexpected win helped to _____ the team's courage.
4. The boss _____ the book at her for having stepped out of line.
5. Teachers often _____ a blind eye to minor breaches of discipline.
6. He's always _____ down his wife's cooking in public.
7. He is very unrealistic and always _____ after rainbows.
8. He _____ me off a strip for having smashed the car.
9. He _____ a real earful from his boss for being late repeatedly.

TASK 2:   What about the adjectives?

At the sports centre, Tom and Ron are discussing their colleague, Pete. Find the right adjective.

Tom: Wow! One eighty! He jumped over that bar as if it were nothing. You should take a leaf out of his book.

Ron: Great! At the office, however, he's not exactly what I'd call a _____ -*flyer* but rather a stick in the mud.

Tom: And he's work-shy, too. It's very _____ *of him* to offer help, when we have almost finished!

Ron: Yes, he's a bit _____ on the uptake. Thinking is not one of his strengths.

Tom: I agree, he's _____ *as a brick.*

TASK 3: On to the animals

Two elderly employees are discussing the new manager. Translate.

Anne: The new one seems to be a (*komischer Vogel*).

Olga: And he behaves like a (*Elephant*) in a china shop towards the young secretaries.

Anne: Did you know that he collects bras. He must have a (*Meise*) in his bonnet about women.

Olga: What annoys me is that he can't admit a mistake. He always tries to pass the (*schwarzen Peter*) to someone else.

TASK 4: Useful objects around the house

Which object fits the idiom best?

1. You needn't show me how to conduct an interview. I've been doing this for ages. *It's like teaching your grandmother to suck _____.*
   A. holes   **B.** screws   **C.** eggs

2. Applicant A was slightly odd in his behaviour, wasn't he? *I think he has a _____ loose.*
   A. screw   **B.** egg   **C.** peg

3. Applicant B's all fingers and thumbs. He would be *like a _____ round our neck.*
   A. millstone   **B.** peg   **C.** candle

4. Applicant C's character and abilities make him not suitable for joining our team. He'd be *a square _____ in a round hole.*
   A. egg   **B.** peg   **C.** millstone

5. However, we should put Applicant D on the short list. The others were not able *to hold a _____ to her.*
   A. egg   **B.** screw   **C.** candle

TASK 5: Definition exercise

Replace the words in *italics* by an idiom that has the same meaning.

1. He was a very creative designer, but as a manager he's *a person of no help or use to anyone.*
2. Her exam results were disappointing, but she *acted as if it was not as bad as it really was.*
3. He's too arrogant – he needs to *be told in no uncertain words that he isn't as important as he thinks he is.*
4. My parents always *disapproved of* my choice of friends.
5. By allowing her to go free the judge *accepted that there was no clear evidence to prove her guilt.*

TASK 6: Matching exercise

1. Express slight approval , suggesting that one does not like them.
2. Accept punishment for something one has not done, in order to protect someone.
3. Remind someone forcefully of the correct way of doing something and perhaps punish them for not following it.
4. Tell them that they have made a mistake.
5. Be determined to oppose someone.
6. Criticize someone severely because they have done something wrong.
7. not outstanding or exceptional; ordinary

A. set one's face against someone
B. throw the book at someone
C. nothing (much) to write home about
D. haul someone over the coals
E. take the rap for something
F. give someone a carpeting
G. damn someone with faint praise

TASK 6: Magic squares – Idioms around the head

Match the phrases (1, 2, 3) with the words in the box (A, B, C). Put the numbers in the magic squares. Columns and rows will all add up to the same number, **15**.

A. ears	D. teeth	G. face
B. neck	E. eye	H. chin
C. nose	F. head	I. lip

1. Keep your ★ up even if it's difficult to remain cheerful in these circumstances.
2. Her remarks really got up my ★!
3. I don't believe a word she said. She's lying through her ★.
4. Your secretary has stepped out of line again. You should pin her ★ back.
5. Bosses often turn a blind ★ to minor breaches of discipline.
6. Keep a stiff upper ★ even though you are in serious trouble.
7. The boss won't bite your ★ off. Barking dogs don't bite.
8. Hide your true feelings, be brave and appear cheerful. Put on a brave ★.
9. You'll get it in the ★ if you're caught stealing.

A =	B =	C =
D =	E =	F =
G =	H =	I =

KEY
SCHLÜSSEL

MODULE 1

TASK 1: Remember our business phrases?

1. He decided to *go it alone*.
2. I'm afraid your automatic hair brush will never *catch on*.
3. Magazines often publish short extracts from new novels to *whet your appetite*.

TASK 2: Odd man out

1. **A.** set up shop – *ein Geschäft / Firma gründen*
2. **A.** kill two birds with one stone – *Zwei Fliegen mit einer Klappe schlagen*
3. **B.** get into a rut – *in den alten Trott fallen*
4. **C.** go downhill – *bergab gehen*

TASK 3: Body language

1. Last year our little grocery was on its last *legs*.
2. We were fighting a losing battle to keep our *heads* above water.
3. We tried everything to get the business onto its *feet* again.
4. However, all of our great ideas to rescue it *bit* the dust!
5. We were up for grabs and almost *swallowed* up by TallWart, a chain of supermarkets.
6. Then the white knight, the software giant SIP, appeared and gave us a *leg* up in the form of a generous loan.

TASK 4: Tim, the 'Yes-man'

1. We mustn't *miss* the *boat*.
2. We're *backing* the wrong *horse*.
3. All the money would *go down the drain*.
4. Yes, the *sands* are *running* out.
5. Yes, indeed a spectacular *U-turn*.
6. Everything here is *going downhill*.
7. Everything here is *on its last legs*.
8. Yes, we'll *go bust*, if we can't find the money.
9. All our projects have clearly *gone up in smoke*.
10. Our company might already *be up for grabs*.
11. We're waiting in vain for a *white knight*.

MODULE 2

TASK 1: Bosses and the kingdom of animals

1. Dr Block is the *fat cat* in our business.
2. He's determined to show that he's still (the) *top dog* in the company.
3. In our small village he is a big *fish*.
4. He thinks he's the *cat's* whiskers.
5. He rules the *roost* because he's the dominant person in the company.
6. Let's see how long he will be able to sit firmly in the *saddle*.

TASK 2: Test your business phrases

1. She appears innocent, although she is probably not.
   She looks as if *butter* wouldn't *melt* in her *mouth*.
2. Let's get down to work:
   Let's *roll* up our *sleeves*.
3. His boss was on a trip, so Peter had to deal with the police.
   Peter was left *holding* the *baby*.

TASK 3: Idioms that make a noise

1. I have no intention of *playing second fiddle* to the new boss, so I'll resign.
2. He has been caught cheating, now he must *face the music*.
3. The children were out in the playground *letting off steam*.
4. You're not the man to *call the tune*. You are not in a position to control the situation.

TASK 4: Magic squares – Body idioms

A = 8	B = 1	C = 6
D = 3	E = 5	F = 7
G = 4	H = 9	I = 2

MODULE 3

TASK 1: What's the opposite?

Tim was given a *golden* handshake.   Tina was given a *leaden* handshake.
Tom has got a *steady job*.   I'm at a *loose end* at the moment.
There are *plenty more fish* in the sea.   Good workers are *far and few between*.
He *dots the "i"s and crosses the "t"s*.   He *has fallen down on the job*.
He always *gives me a rough ride*.   He always *praises Bob to the skies*.

TASK 2: Odd man out

1. **B.** It's on my way.
2. **A.** separate the black cats from the white ones.
3. **C.** Ok, let's draw numbers.
4. **A.** He gave us a good shampoo.
5. **B.** 300 hundred got their walking cards.

TASK 3: Streamline your English

1. She writes well enough, but she *can't hold a candle to* the more serious novelists.
2. Our plans are now well advanced so I need to *put you in the picture* about the project.
3. She's just joined the department – it'll take a week or two to *show her the ropes*.
4. He's *a dab hand at* programming.
5. You'll have to *get your act together*, if you want to pass the exam.
6. I was *short-listed for the job*, but I didn't get it.

TASK 4: Assonance and alliteration

1. It's really scraping the *bottom* of the *barrel* ...
2. The sunny intervals ... have been *few and far* between.
3. About 10 percent of trainees fail to *make the grade*.
4. You can't make a *silk* purse out of a *sow's* ear.
5. The new chairman was given a *rough ride*.

TASK 5: Magic squares – Animal idioms

A = 6	B = 7	C = 2
D = 1	E = 5	F = 9
G = 8	H = 3	I = 4

MODULE 4

TASK 1: Those nasty little words

1. He's been here for years and should know the *ins* and *outs* of the job by now.
2. If you want to pass that exam, you'll have to knuckle *down*.
3. The airline pulled *out* all the stops to get him there *in* time.
4. I've been swamped *with* work this year.

TASK 2: Clean up the mess

1. Already at the age of 18 he *carved* out his *career*.
2. His aim was to get into the *room* at the *top*.
3. However, he refused to *play second fiddle* to anyone.
4. Little wonder that *fell* from *grace*.

TASK 3: Idioms with a 'c'

1. Tom is a lazy bones; he usually *conks* out for an hour or so after his lunch break.
2. When I asked him how the exam was, he replied "It was a *cinch*!"
3. Tom is extremely unrealistic. He's always building *castles* in the air.
4. That is why Tom tends to bite off more than he can *chew*.
5. Now Tom is thinking of *carving* out a name for himself as a golf trainer.

TASK 4: What's the woggle?

1. She's an expert tax consultant. She knows her *onions*.
2. He made her his personal assistant. That girl plays her *cards* right.
3. We do all the *donkey*-work and the boss takes the credit!
4. I've been working my fingers to the *bone* to build this house and now she refuses to move in with me.
5. Don't interfere with my project. It's my *baby*!

TASK 5: Idioms from the world of crafts

1. My debts were like a *millstone* round my neck.
2. First things first. Don't put the *cart* before the horse
3. This is sabotage! He's always trying to throw a *spanner* in the works.
4. The boss promised me promotion if I keep my nose to the *grindstone*.
5. Tina is very efficient. She has been with us for only two months and has already learned the *ropes*.
6. They heard the offer. Then they downed *tools*.

TASK 6: Magic squares – Body idioms

A = 6	B = 7	C = 2
D = 1	E = 5	F = 9
G = 8	H = 3	I = 4

MODULE 5

TASK 1: Missing letters (they are all vowels)

1. We've already *ploughed* too much money into this old house.
2. Who's going to *foot* the bill for all the repairs?
3. I'm afraid we won't even be able to *cover* the costs of the new roof.
4. We must somehow *raise* money for the repairs. This house is worth it.

TASK 2: Those nasty little words

1. Tom gave me a tip-off! Buy Bayer! It's *as* safe *as* houses, he said.
2. I came *within* an inch of selling my shares *at* an all-time-high.
3. You should have got *out while* the going was good.
4. Well, the next day the bottom had fallen *out of* the stock market.

TASK 3: They have almost the same meaning

1. be up to one's eyes in debt   be up to the *hilt* in debt
2. not have a red cent   not have two *pennies* to *rub* together
3. just manage to scrape together enough money to make a living   make *both* ends *meet*

TASK 4: At the fortune teller's

1. No, you'll be in the *red.*
2. No, we'll get a *bearish* market.
3. No, you're backing a *loser.*
4. No, they'll *sky-rocket* again.

TASK 5: Tim, the 'Yes-man'

1. Yes, the bottom has *fallen* out of the *market.*
2. Yes, good old Jenny has *feathered* her nest.
3. Yes, indeed, this publication brought her a nice *windfall.*
4. Yes, he seems to be *gambling in* oil shares.
5. I agree, it's high time that he *cut* his *losses.*
6. They are obviously beginning to *feel* the *pinch.*

TASK 6: Odd man out

1. **B.** When are you going to cook the books? (die Bilanz / Bücher fälschen)
2. **B.** I'm afraid we've *touched rock bottom* (den Tiefpunkt erreicht)
3. **A.** the old woman is on the breadline (am Hungertuch nagen)

TASK 7: Magic squares – The animal world

A = 6	B = 1	C = 8
D = 7	E = 5	F = 3
G = 2	H = 9	I = 4

MODULE 6

TASK 1: | Let's go woggling again

L: Somehow your work seems to have *got* off on the wrong *foot*. The results aren't satisfactory.

E: I know. I've drawn a *blank* with almost every project. I feel like I'm having a rough ride in my new job.

TASK 2: | Get your idioms right

E: We got a chance to *open* up new *fields*, and it means our copiers will remain *state* of the *art*.

F: That might well be, but we're getting beyond our budget.

E: But you have to have vision. I feel I'm *beating* my head against a *brick wall.* Let me try to explain ...

TASK 3: | Fill in the blanks

S: And our copier produces three thousand copies an hour. That *breaks* all *records*.

C: Very good, but the *acid* test is whether the copies are in usable quality.

S: The technology is *brand* new and this guarantees excellent print quality.

C: I must say that your last product caused a lot of problems. We had to lick the machine into *shape*.

S: Of course, it's no good *crying* over *spilt* milk.

TASK 4: | Tom, the 'Yes-man'

1. Yes, we've been *racking* our *brains* trying to find something.
2. You're right, you can't make *bricks* without *straw*.
3. Yes, it's all *hit-and-miss* experimentation.
4. Yes, they expect us to *take* the *rap*.
5. Yes, what we need is a *brain wave*.

TASK 5: Magic squares

A = 2	B = 7	C = 6
D = 9	E = 5	F = 1
G = 4	H = 3	I = 8

MODULE 7

TASK 1: Odd man out

1. **C.** gift-wrap – als Geschenk verpacken
2. **A.** It's a snip. – Es ist ein Schnäppchen
3. **B.** they cost next to nothing – sie kosten so viel wie nichts
4. **C.** It used to be their shelf-warmer – Es war ihr Ladenhüter.

TASK 2: Make up your mind

1. I was foolish enough to (**A**) *fall for it.*
2. If I'd been offered it, I'd have (**B**) *jumped at it.*
3. I had to (**A**) *pay up front.*
4. She didn't pay me all at once but (**B**) *in dribs and drabs.*
5. Tourists complain of being (**A**) *ripped off* by local taxi-drivers.

TASK 3: Find the opposite

Harry Potter books are *good sellers.*

The self-help book 'All I know about women' is a *shelf-warmer.*

Cigarettes must be paid *up front.*

Cars may be bought on *HP* (*hire purchase.*

Tourists hope to *be given a square deal.*

In some countries, however, they *are* often *ripped off.*

Some tourists *lose their cool* when they are fleeced.

But they quickly *cool down* again over a good glass of wine.

TASK 4: | Tim, the 'Yes-man'

1. Property prices have gone *through the roof*.
2. Yes, she thinks it's the *chance* of a *lifetime*.
3. She'll pay *through the nose* for a house in that area.
4. The repairs will cost *an arm* and *a leg*.
5. Her fiancé must have *railroaded* her into buying it.
6. Yes, they will sell her *a white elephant*.

TASK 5: | Magic squares – Animals and textiles

A = 6	B = 1	C = 8
D = 7	E = 5	F = 3
G = 2	H = 9	I = 4

MODULE 8

TASK 1: | Say it with an idiom

1. *narrow* the agenda *down*
2. *take* the *minutes*
3. give the *floor* to someone
4. speak *off* the *record*

TASK 2: | Tom, the chairman, and Tim, the 'Yes-man'

1. Yes, I think you should *run / chair the meeting*.
2. Okay, let the meeting *roll*.
3. Okay, let's get *down* to *brass tacks*.
4. Yes, let's talk about the budget *for openers*.
5. Yes, we've *covered a lot of ground*.
6. Yes, let's *call it a day*.

TASK 3: | Which idiom suits the context best

1. Pete has been talking for hours boring everybody.(**A.**) He can talk the hind legs off a donkey.

2. The committee is considering the proposal and we're waiting to see (**C.**) which side of the fence it comes down on.

3. They have failed to decide between courses of action, because they are afraid to offend the directors. (**C.**) They are sitting on the fence.

4. Although the director has retired, he tries to be up-to-date. (**B.**) He reads all the minutes and that keeps him in the swim.

5. We've covered all the topics so let's (**B.**) wind the meeting up.

TASK 4: | Letter mix-up

1. Contributing to the success of a meeting is not as *simple* as that.

2. If you're out of luck the chairperson will ask you to *keep* the *minutes*.

3. Most of the time participants *talk* at cross-*purposes*.

4. If the participants speak all at the same time the chairperson will *call* them to *order*.

5. And if you speak out of *turn* the chairperson will *rule* you out of order.

TASK 5: | Odd man out

1. A. It's clear as water (völlig klar sein)

2. B. be far and few between (dünn gesät sein)

3. C. be old hat (ein alter Hut sein)

4. B. on the agenda (auf der Tagesordnung stehen)

5. A. He's out of place (fehl am Platz, unangebracht sein)

TASK 6: | Business phrases to remember

1. The first item on the *agenda* is whether we shall *grant* discount for *quantity*.

2. I think it's a bit early for a decision. I move for *adjournment*.

3. I suggest that we *appoint* a subcommittee.

4. Let's have a *vote* on this *item*.

TASK 7: Magic squares – Around the house

A = 4	B = 3	C = 8
D = 9	E = 5	F = 1
G = 2	H = 7	I = 6

MODULE 9

TASK 1: Idioms in poem

I tried to clear the *way*
For an agreement – cost what it *may*.
They gambled on the *enterprise*
Refused to strike a *compromise*.
Finally I had to *beat*
A disappointed slow *retreat*.

TASK 2: You keep it in your fridge

1. He's always as cool as a *cucumber*.
2. I don't put all my *eggs* into one basket.
3. He can't have his *cake* and eat it!
4. You can't just pick the *cherries* from the cake.
5. This proposal is a very different kettle of *fish*.
6. The quality you're offering us now is as different as chalk and *cheese* from the one you sent us a week ago.

TASK 3: Idioms from the animal world

1. I'll try to put out some *feelers* to test people's reactions to the idea.
2. I'm afraid we bet on the wrong *horse*.
3. A *bird* in the hand is worth two in the bush.
4. You can talk till the *cows* come home.
5. Let's wait and see which way the *cat* jumps.
6. He could talk the hind legs off a *donkey*.

TASK 4: | Rhyme Verbs

1. Don't *play* a waiting game. *Lay* your cards on the table.
2. Don't *sit* on the fence and *split* hairs.
3. When you *meet* your match, you'd better *beat* a retreat.
4. He *burned* his bridges and *turned* up trumps.
5. Don't *blow* hot and cold – *show* your colours.

TASK 5: | The good negotiator and clothes

1. A good negotiator never aims below the *belt*.
2. He is able to put himself in his partner's *shoes*.
3. You'll never catch him with his *trousers* down.
4. It's very difficult to have him in your *pocket*.

TASK 6: | Magic squares – They grow on your body

A = 6	B = 7	C = 2
D = 1	E = 5	F = 9
G = 8	H = 3	I = 4

MODULE 10

TASK 1: | Do you remember the idiom?

1. **C.** The market place for new anti aging-drugs is nothing more than a *free-for-all*.
2. **C.** The publication of the test results of the drug Viagry caught the pharmaceutical company ABS *on the hop*.
3. **A.** The ABS went to great *lengths* to keep the test results secret.
4. **C.** Some managers, who had a bad conscience about the by-effects of Viagry, gained the *upper hand*.
5. **B.** Finally, the Board *threw in the towel* and withdrew the drug from the market.

TASK 2: Which idiom goes with which definition?

1. come / get to grips with something = **F.** begin to deal seriously with a problem, challenge, etc
2. turn the tables on someone = **E.** reverse a situation so as to put oneself in a position of superiority
3. jockey for a position = **D.** try by every available means to gain an advantage or a favour
4. wipe the floor with someone = **C.** defeat someone thoroughly in an argument or a contest
5. keep one jump ahead of someone = **B.** remain one stage ahead of a rival
6. hold one's own against = **A.** maintain one's position against competition and not become weaker

---

TASK 3: Say it in English

1. Last year we *mounted an advertising campaign* for our new electric scooter for kids.
2. It was the first scooter of its kind and so we *got a head start on* our competitors.
3. However, FwS (Fun with Sun) developed a scooter driven by solar energy and *gained a foothold* on the market.
4. At first we were able *to hold our own against* FwS.
5. But soon we felt *them breathing down our neck.*
6. It was an extremely hot and sunny year so little by little FwS *got the edge over us.*
7. In order not to *be out of the running* we're developing a skate board propelled by solar energy.
8. And if we manage to integrate the solar cells in a T-shirt we'll *beat FwS hollow*, I bet my bottom dollar on it.

TASK 4: Tim, the 'Yes-man'

1. **Tim:** Of course, we'll *be one jump ahead* of them.
2. **Tim:** Of course, they'll be *out of the running.*
3. **Tim:** Yes, we'll *beat them hollow*, that's for sure.
4. **Tim:** Yes, we'll *wipe them off the map.*

<table>
<tr><td>TASK 5:</td><td>Magic squares – Sporting idioms</td></tr>
</table>

A = 2	B = 9	C = 4
D = 7	E = 5	F = 3
G = 6	H = 1	I = 8

MODULE 11

<table>
<tr><td>TASK 1:</td><td>Colourful idioms</td></tr>
</table>

1. You'll lose you driver's license if you go through a *red* light again.
2. Politicians seem to get away with *blue* murder in this country.
3. We'll have to wait until we get the judgement in *black* and *white*.
4. The muggers beat the young tourist *black* and *blue*.
5. Don't let the police catch you *red*-handed.

<table>
<tr><td>TASK 2:</td><td>Tim, the 'Yes-man'</td></tr>
</table>

1. Tim: Yes, its unfair that it's always you who has to *face the music*.
2. Tim: That's it. We must *catch* him *red-handed*.
3. Tim: Of course, we'll *take him to court* immediately.

<table>
<tr><td>TASK 3:</td><td>Odd man out</td></tr>
</table>

1. A. bump someone off: jemanden um die Ecke bringen
2. C. keep a stiff upper lip: Haltung bewahren
3. B. come clean about it: ein Geständnis ablegen
4. C. get a dose of one's own medicine: etwas am eigenen Leib verspüren
5. A. get his come-uppance: seine wohlverdiente Strafe erhalten

TASK 4: Verbs that go with law

1. The director ... was determined to *go to law* ...
2. Ron fled to Brazil trying to *evade the law*, ...
3. He ... was surprised to find out that Brazilian judges *stick to the letter of the law*.
4. ... Ron's lawyer tried to *bend ... the law* ...

TASK 5: Magic squares – Body idioms

A = 2	B = 9	C = 4
D = 7	E = 5	F = 3
G = 6	H = 1	I = 8

MODULE 12

TASK 1: Do you remember?

1. We've had flooding all week and it's still *bucketing down*.
2. The files for the seminar got *wet through* in the rain.
3. Anne's so sensitive. She's *got goose pimples* three quarters of the year.

TASK 2: Idioms for alcoholics

1. I know it's early, but I'll *wet my whistle* in any case. I'm thirsty.
2. Tom got a headache. I guess he had *a drop too much* last night.
3. We've won the lottery. Let's go out and *paint the town red*.

TASK 3: What do you say?

1. It's your uncle's birthday. *"Many happy returns!"*
2. You meet the boss on January 1st. *"Happy New Year!"*
3. You visit Tom in hospital. *"I wish you a speedy recovery."*
4. You raise your glass of champagne. *"To your good health!"*

TASK 4: | Incompatible characters

I think she *looks* rather *like death warmed up*.
What? He's *enough to make me want to puke (sl)*.
Stag party? You mean *'hen party'*.
I hate parties. I'm the born *wallflower*.
Nonsense! I'd *be bored out of my mind*.

TASK 5: | Tim, the 'Yes-man'

1. Yes, *he's a chip off the old block*.
2. Yes, it was *a shot-gun marriage*.
3. Yes, this marriage has *set a lot of tongues wagging*. *It's the talk of the town*.
4. Yes, she's *flinging dirt* at Freddy.
5. Yes, he *rubs shoulders* with all the important people at the Town Hall.

TASK 6: | Magic squares – The animal world

A = 2	B = 9	C = 4
D = 7	E = 5	F = 3
G = 6	H = 1	I = 8

MODULE 13

TASK 1: | Odd man out

1. **C.** Yes, he doesn't stick to his guns (auf seinem Standpunkt beharren).
2. **B.** No, he's still caught between the devil and the deep blue sea (in der Zwickmühle stecken).
3. **A.** Yes, he might be on shaky ground (sich auf unsicherem Terrain bewegen).

TASK 2: | Why Tim will not climb the ladder

1. He's always *barking up the wrong tree.*
2. And as soon as he has found the right tree *he saws off the branch he's sitting on.*
3. In meetings he always *gets hold of the wrong end of the stick.*
4. He's thinking about resigning – if he resigns *he will have burnt his boats* and he might regret it.
5. Tim *cannot see the wood* for the *trees.*

TASK 3: | Metallic idioms

1. *He stuck to his guns.*
2. *He's always putting his two cents in.*
3. *I'm on a knife-edge about the results.*
4. He ... *was jumping out of the frying-pan* into the fire.

TASK 4: | Time for a rhyme

Caught between the devil and the deep blue *sea?*
No! I think you're barking up the wrong *tree.*
Don't bury your head anymore in the *sand.*
Roll up your sleeves and take a *stand.*
Take stock, change track and *tack.*
Louder than words speak actions.
Wake up and make decisions.
Weigh up the pros and *cons.*
And stick to your *guns.*
My son!

TASK 5: | Tim, the 'Yes-man'

1. Yes, let's release a press statement to *put the record straight.*
2. Yes, we must *drive that message home.*
3. Right, they *haven't a leg to stand on.*
4. Yes, I certainly won't *pull my punches.*
5. Yes, let's *nail our colours to the mast.*

TASK 6: Remember our business phrases?

1. appreciate someone's opinions: jemandes Meinung zu schätzen wissen
2. expand on the home market: auf dem Binnenmarkt expandieren
3. he hasn't performed: er hat nichts geleistet
4. I should have a rise: ich sollte eine Gehaltserhöhung bekommen
5. transfer someone to Libya: jemanden nach Libyen versetzen

TASK 7: Do you remember the German?

Caught between the devil and the deep blue *sea*?
in einer Zwickmühle stecken
I think you're barking up the wrong *tree*.
auf dem Holzweg sein
Don't bury your head in the *sand*.
den Kopf in den Sand stecken
Roll up your sleeves and take a *stand*.
Ärmel aufkrempeln, Stellung beziehen
Weigh up the pros and *cons*
das Für und Wider abwägen
And stick to your *guns*.
auf seinem Standpunkt beharren

MODULE 14

TASK 1: Dynamic verbs of movement

1. Things are progressing well – please don't do anything to *rock* the boat.
2. I was *hauled* over the coals by my boss for being late.
3. The unexpected win helped to *boost* the team's courage.
4. The boss *threw* the book at her for having stepped out of line.
5. Teachers often *turn* a blind eye to minor breaches of discipline.
6. He's always *running* down his wife's cooking in public.
7. He is very unrealistic and always *chasing* after rainbows.

8. He *tore* me off a strip for having smashed the car.
9. He *caught* a real earful from his boss for being late repeatedly.

TASK 2: What about the adjectives?

Tom: Wow! One eighty! You should take a leaf out of his book.

Ron: Great! At the office, however, he's not exactly what I'd call a *high-flyer* but rather a stick in the mud.

Tom: And he's work-shy, too. It's very *big of* him to offer help, when we have almost finished!

Ron: Yes, he's a bit *slow* on the uptake. Thinking is not one of his strengths.

Tom: I agree, he's *as thick* as a brick.

TASK 3: On to the animals

Anne: The new one seems to be a *gay /queer bird*.

Olga: And he behaves like a *bull* in a china shop towards the young secretaries.

Anne: Did you know that he collects bras. He must have a *bee* in his bonnet about women.

Olga: What annoys me is that he can't admit a mistake. He always tries to pass the *buck* to someone else.

TASK 4: Useful objects around the house

1. *It's like teaching your grandmother to suck* (C.) *eggs*.
2. *I think he has a* (A.) *screw loose*.
3. He would be *like a* (A.) *millstone round our neck*.
4. He'd be *a square* (B.) *peg in a round hole*.
5. The others were not able *to hold a* (C.) *candle to* her.

TASK 5: Definition exercise

1. He was a very creative designer, but as a manager he's *a dead loss* (a person of no help or use to anyone).
2. Her exam results were disappointing but she tried to *put a brave face on* it (acted as if it was not as bad as it really was).

3. He's too arrogant – he needs to *be taken down a peg or two* (be told in no uncertain words that he isn't as important as he thinks he is).
4. My parents always *frowned on* (disapproved of) my choice of friends.
5. By allowing her to go free the judge gave the accused the *benefit of the doubt* (accepted that there was no clear evidence to prove her guilt).

TASK 6: matching exercise

1. **G.** Express slight approval, suggesting that one does not like them: *damn someone with faint praise*
2. **E.** Accept punishment for something one has not done, in order to protect someone: *take the rap for something*
3. **B.** Remind someone forcefully of the correct way of doing something and perhaps punish them for not following it: *throw the book at someone*
4. **F.** Tell them that they have made a mistake: *give someone a carpeting*
5. **A.** Be determined to oppose someone: *set one's face against someone*
6. **D.** Criticize someone severely because they have done something wrong: *haul someone over the coals*
7. **C.** Not outstanding or exceptional; ordinary: *nothing (much) to write home about*

TASK 7: Magic squares – Idioms around the head

A = 4	B = 9	C = 2
D = 3	E = 5	F = 7
G = 8	H = 1	I = 6

Meet the international
business world with
Let's Go International *Business
English rund um die Welt*
(Buch: rororo 60267 /
Buch mit Audio-CD:
rororo 60504 /
Toncassette: 60505)

Words, words, words –
pick and choose the
right one with
Bryan Hemming
Business English from A to Z
*Wörter und Wendungen für
alle Situationen*
(rororo 60269)

Know where
you're in business
English with
Check Your Language Level
*Business English auf dem
Prüfstand*
(rororo 60268)

The world of
technology for
the businessman
The Way Things Work
*Technisches Englisch für
Business und Alltag*
(rororo 60369)

Know what to say
and how to say it
Small Talk for Big Business
*Business Conversation für
bessere Kontakte*
(rororo 60439)

Help yourself
to sell in English
Sell like Hell *Business English
für Verkaufsgespräche*
(rororo 60722)

RENÉ BOSEWITZ / ROBERT KLEINSCHROTH

SPICE UP
YOUR SPEECHES
RHETORIK
FÜR ALLE GESCHÄFTSANLÄSSE

rororo

The right phrase
for all situations
Master Your Business Phrases
*Sprachmodule für den
Geschäftsalltag*
(rororo 60725)

English phrases for
the whole company
**Get to Grips with Company
English** *Wortschatztraining
on the Job*
(rororo 60845)

Don't panic,
win your audience
Spice up Your Speeches
*Rhetorik für alle
Geschäftsanlässe*
(Buch: rororo 60804 /
Buch mit Audio-CD:
rororo 60843 /
Toncassette: rororo 60844)

Weitere Informationen in der
Rowohlt Revue, kostenlos in
Ihrer Buchhandlung, oder im
Internet: www.rororo.de

Uwe Kreisel /
Pamela Ann Tabbert
Multilingua Englisch *von Anfang an*
(Buch: rororo sachbuch 60481 / Buch mit Audio-CD: rororo sachbuch 60435 / Toncassette: rororo sachbuch 60482)

Uwe Kreisel
Flüssiges Englisch *Mit Redensarten zu mehr Eloquenz*
(rororo sachbuch 61183)

Ronald Lister /
Klemens Veth
Idioms im Griff *Phrasal Verbs, Redewendungen und Metaphern nach Situationen*
(rororo sachbuch 60507)

Emer O'Sullivan /
Dietmar Rösler
Modern Talking *Englisches Quasselbuch mit Sprüchen und Widersprüchen*
(rororo sachbuch 18427)

Ernest Pasakarnis
Master your Idioms *Der Schlüssel zu den englischen Redewendungen*
(rororo sachbuch 18491)

Weitere Informationen in der **Rowohlt Revue**, kostenlos im Buchhandel, und im **Internet:** **www.rororo.de**

3668/4

Robert Kleinschroth
Sprachen lernen *Der Schlüssel
zur richtgen Technik*
(rororo 60842)

Gunther Bischoff
Speak you English?
*Programmierte Übung
zum Verlernen typisch
deutscher Englischfehler*
(rororo 16857)
Better Times *Ein leichtes
Programm zum richtigen
Gebrauch der englischen
Zeiten*
(rororo 17987)

René Bosewitz
Better Your English *Wie man
typisch deutsche Fehler
verlernt*
(rororo 60802)
Perfect Your English *Wie man
die tückischsten
Sprachfallen vermeidet*
(rororo 61147)

René Bosewitz /
Robert Kleinschroth
Joke by Joke to Conversation
*Sprechsituationen mit Witz
gemeistert*
(rororo 18797)
**Joke Your Way Through English
Grammar** *Wichtige Regeln
zum Anlachen*
(rororo 18527)

Hartmut Breitkreuz
False Friends *Stolpersteine
des deutsch-englischen
Wortschatzes*
(rororo 18492)

Hartmut Breitkreuz /
René Bosewitz
**Getting on Top of Idiomatic
Verbs** *Tausend Wendungen
im Kontext*
(rororo 18523)

Iain Galbraith / Paul Krieger
Englisch in letzter Minute *Ein
Sprachführer für Kurz-
entschlossene*
(Buch: rororo 60908 /
Buch mit Audio-CD:
rororo 60909 /
Toncassette: rororo 60910)

Hans-Georg Heuber
**Talk one's head off. Ein Loch in
den Bauch reden** *Englische
Redewendungen und ihre
deutschen «opposite
numbers»*
(rororo 17653)

Weitere Informationen in der
Rowohlt Revue, kostenlos im
Buchhandel, und im **Internet:**
www.rororo.de

rororo sprachen

Die **Überflieger** sind der Einstieg für alle, denen ein ganzes Lehrbuch zu langwierig und ein Sprachführer zu floskelhaft ist. Mit der ausgefeilten Methode der "Überflieger" können Sie schon in wenigen Tagen die notwendigen Grundkenntnisse erwerben, um sich in einem fremden Land zu verständigen. Praktische Tips zu Kultur und Alltag helfen bei der Orientierung.

Uwe Kreisel /
Pamela Ann Tabbert
American Slang in letzter Minute
(Buch: rororo 19623 /
Toncassette: rororo 19705)

Iain Galbraith / Paul Krieger
Englisch in letzter Minute
(Buch: rororo 60908 /
Buch mit Audio-CD:
rororo 60909 /
Toncassette: rororo 60910)

Isabelle Jue /
Nicole Zimmermann
Französisch in letzter Minute
(Buch: rororo 60911 /
Buch mit Audio-CD:
rororo 60912 /
Toncassette: rororo 60913)

Frida Bordon /
Giuseppe Siciliano
Italienisch in letzter Minute
(Buch: rororo 60914 /
Buch mit Audio-CD:
rororo 60915 /
Toncassette: rororo 60916)

Christof Kehr
Spanisch in letzter Minute
(Buch: rororo 60917 /
Buch mit Audio-CD:
rororo 60918 /
Toncassette: rororo 60919)

Weitere Informationen in der **Rowohlt Revue**, kostenlos im Buchhandel, und im **Internet:** **www.rororo.de**

rororo sprachen